Volume 3 of the Inspired Art Coloring Books Series

Allot of my art is inspired by my experience with the environment around me. I like asking people what kind of animals they like, or being mindful of the places I hang out at, or even seeing the exquisiteness in a flowering tree. The world is an amazing place. I hope that you find my images as beautiful as I do, while creating them.

My art style was inspired by the old method of creating silk screens over 25 years ago. Depending on your background, culture, or mind set, you might see something completely different within each image. You may even notice a different image than what I actually intended, finding wonderful hidden treasures within each piece itself.

It is amazing that we can create such incredible images out of different parts and pieces. That our minds can connect individual lines and merge them into amazing ensembles of art. As my style continued to develop, it became the way I see the energy and flow of the world. An under lying base of life. People have seen many different cultural and artistic influences from around the world in my art. When colored, it can take on the look of stained glass. It makes my heart warm when I hear all the different things people see in my style.

You will find many of the pieces emphasize negative space. In each image the negative space is just as important as the positive space. When coloring, allow yourself to explore both inside and outside the lines with a variety of hues. Let the colors flow naturally, in a way that feels right to you. There is no wrong or right way to color.

The last page has all art listed with what the main image is of. But don't look at it until you decide what each art piece is first. Because you might see something very different and that is wonderful.

Each page can be cut out and framed so you can display your colored creations.

The art is printed on one side of the paper.

Recommend using cardstock or multiple sheets of paper to stop bleed-through to the next page. You can test on the last few pages in the book.

Happy coloring,

Brian Scott

ISBN: 1530358876   ISBN-13: 978-1530358878

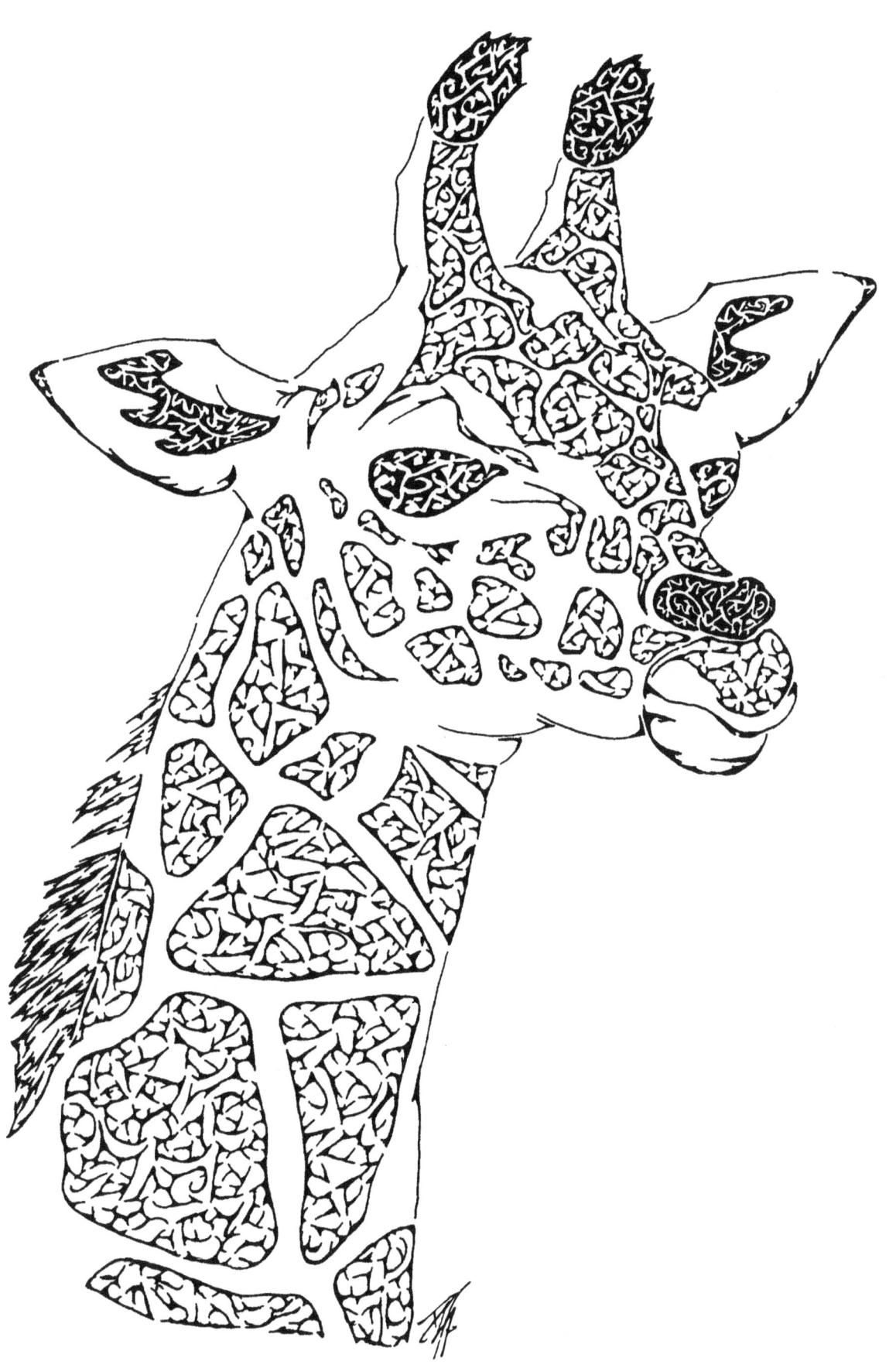

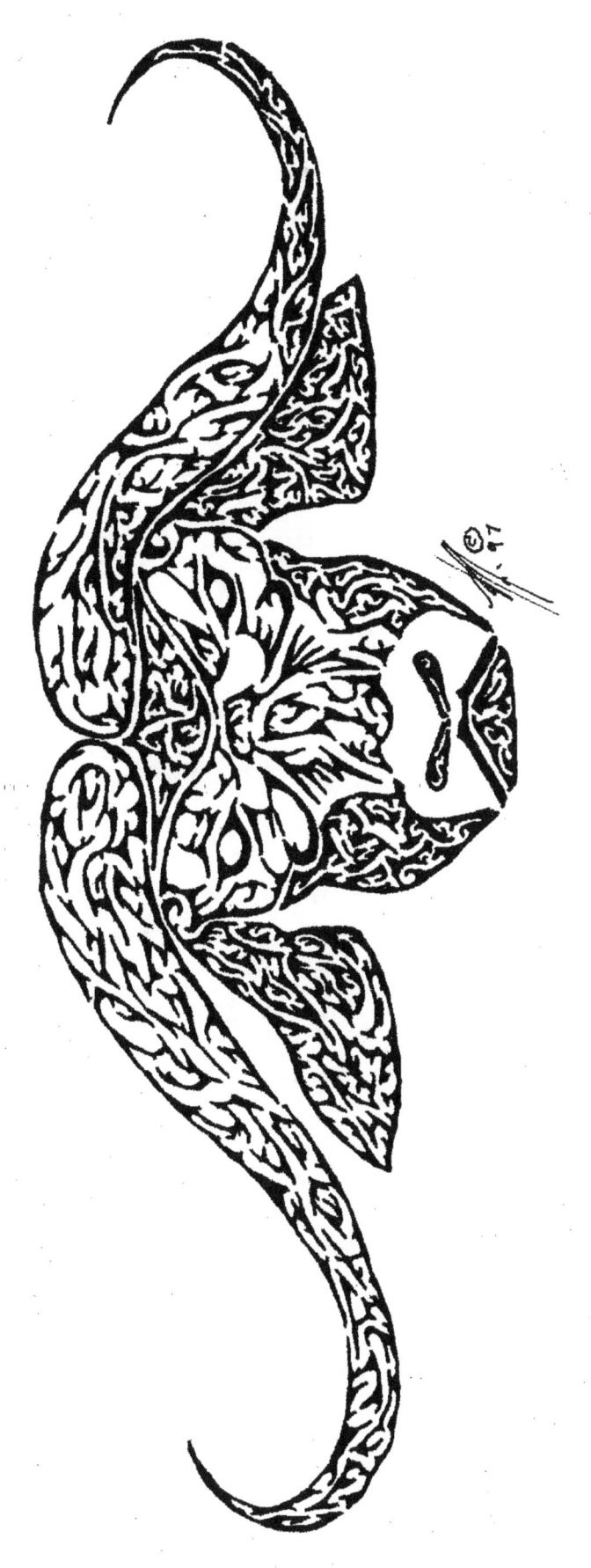

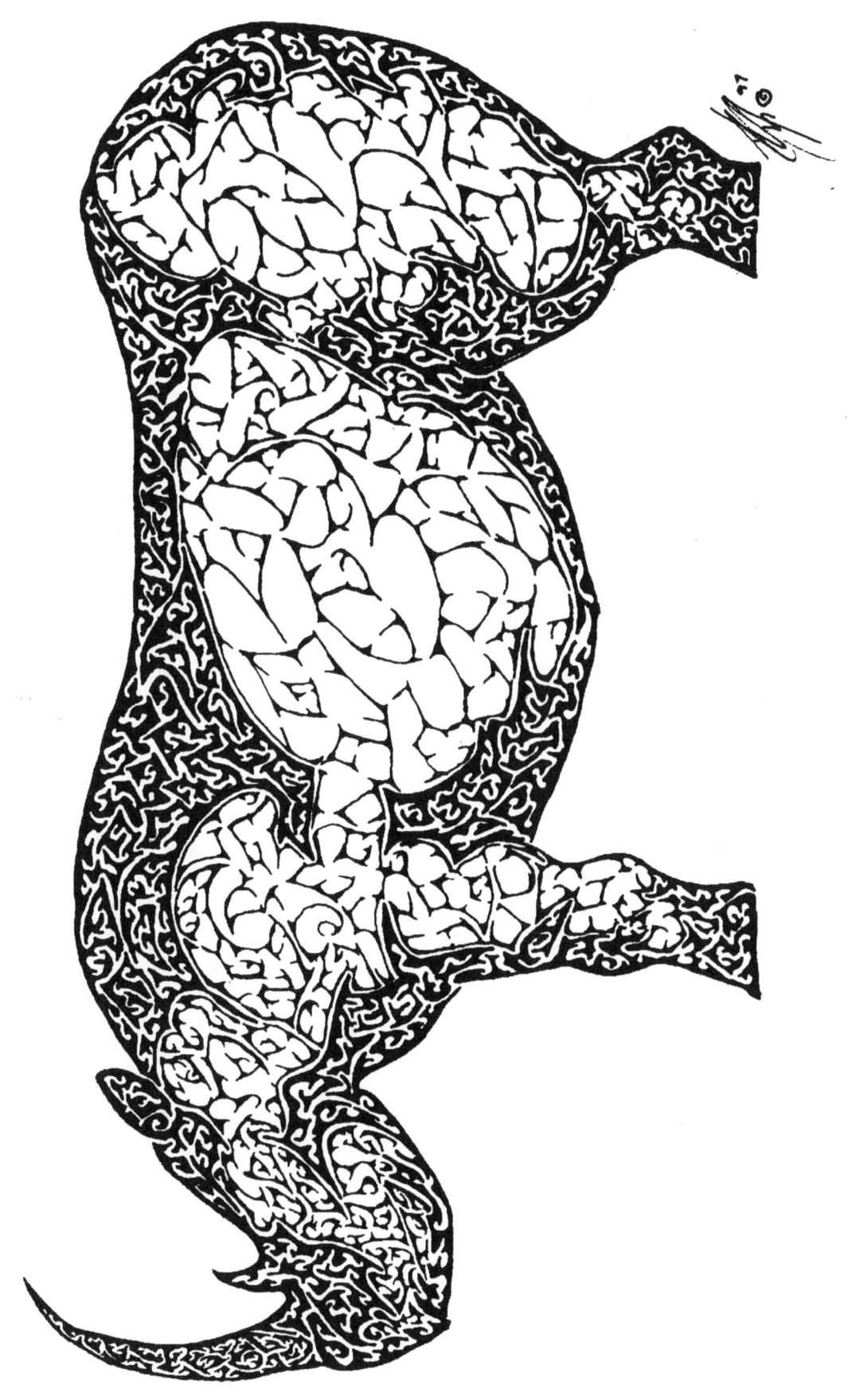

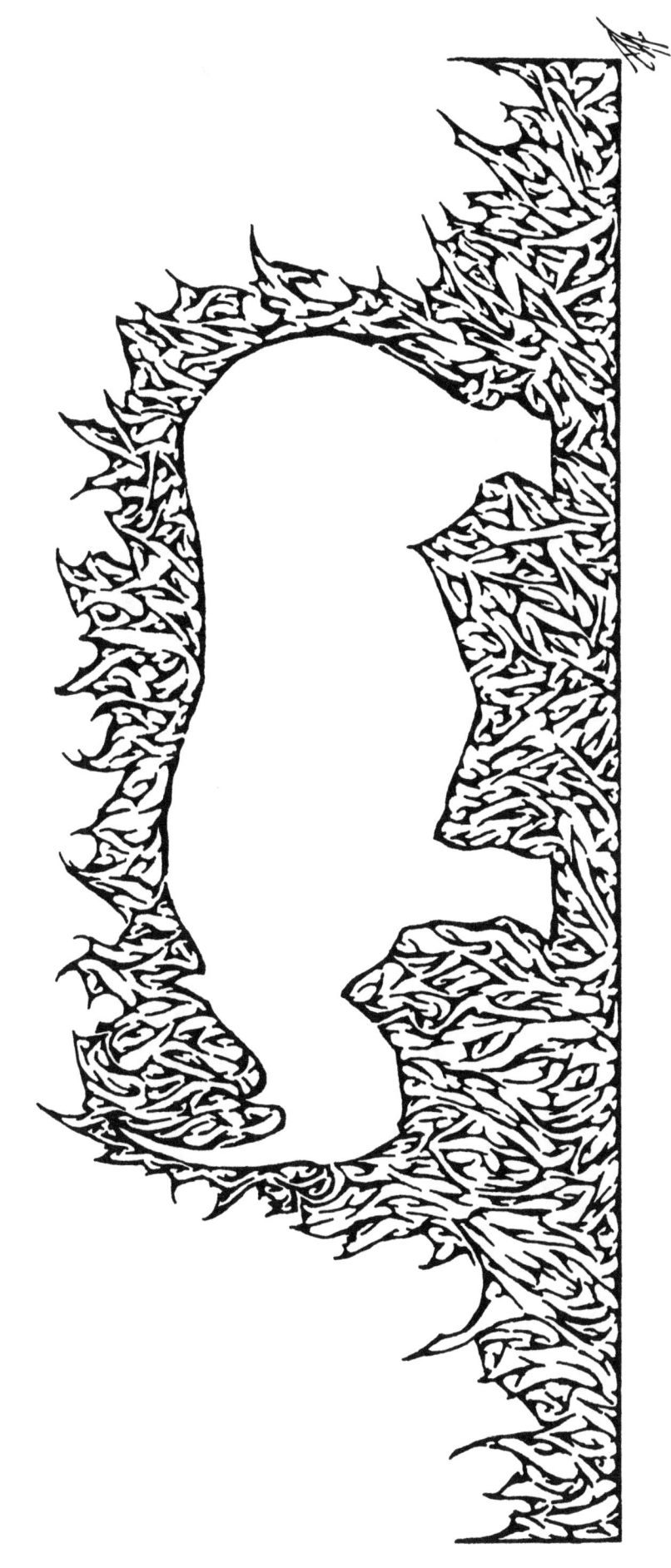

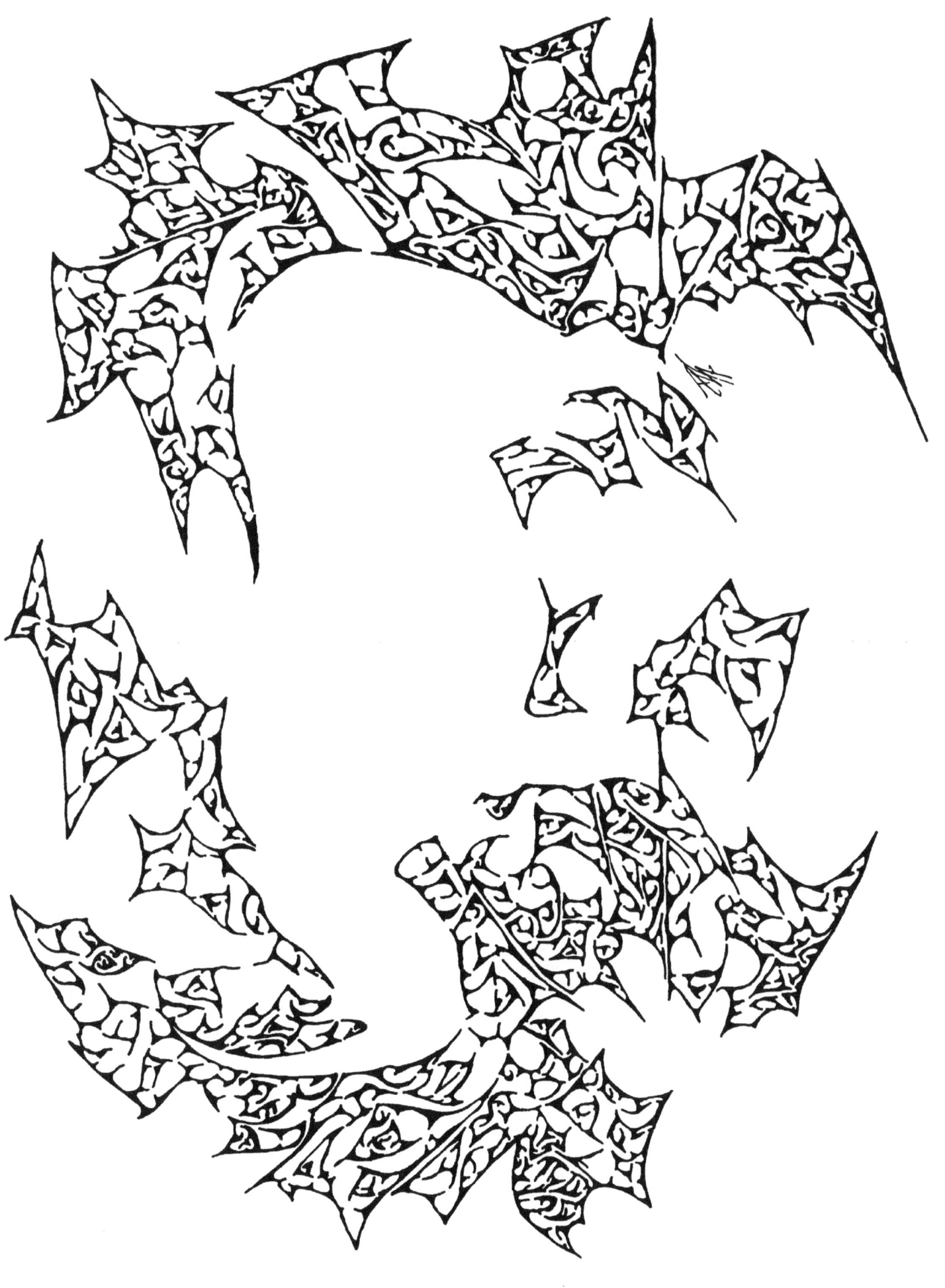

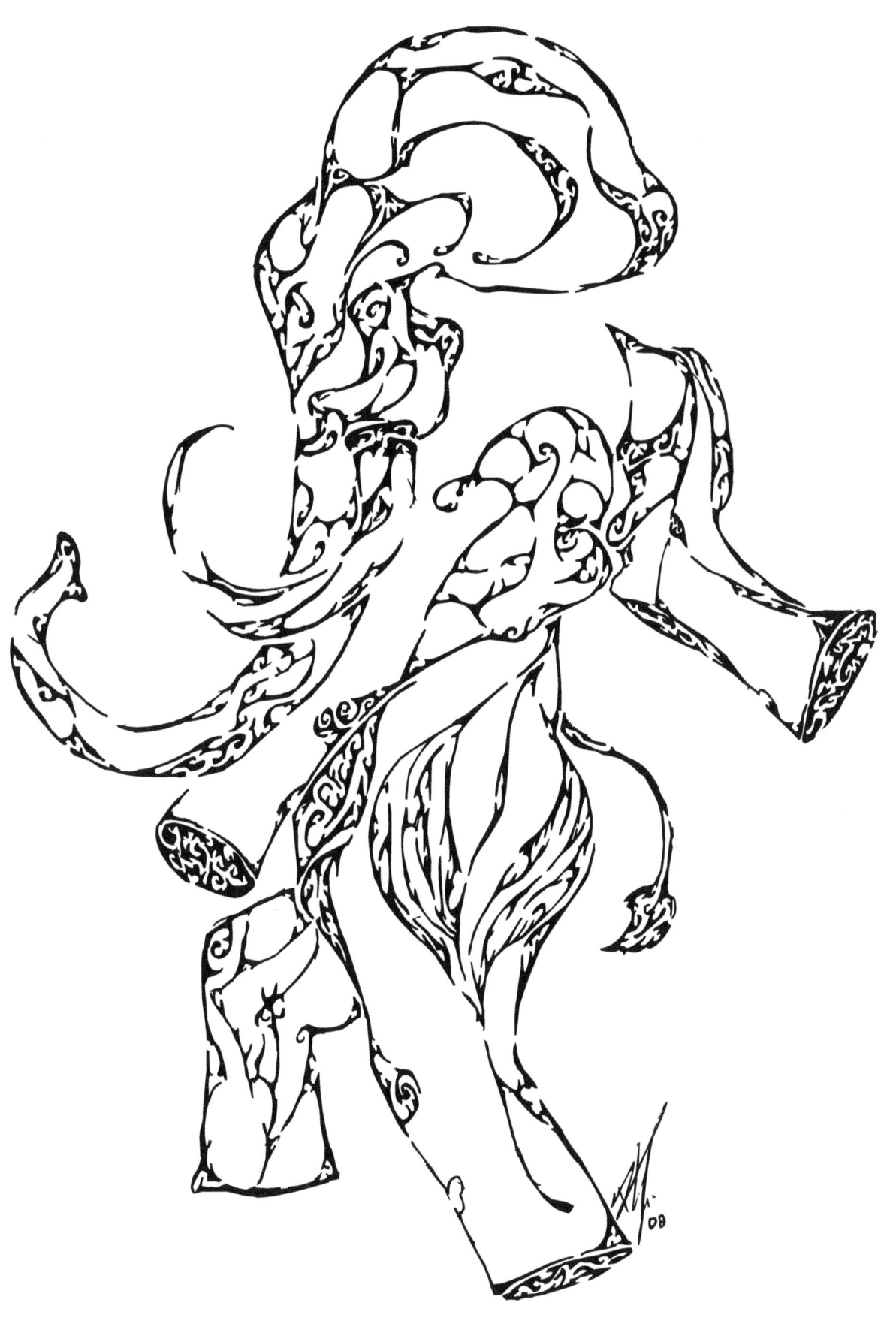

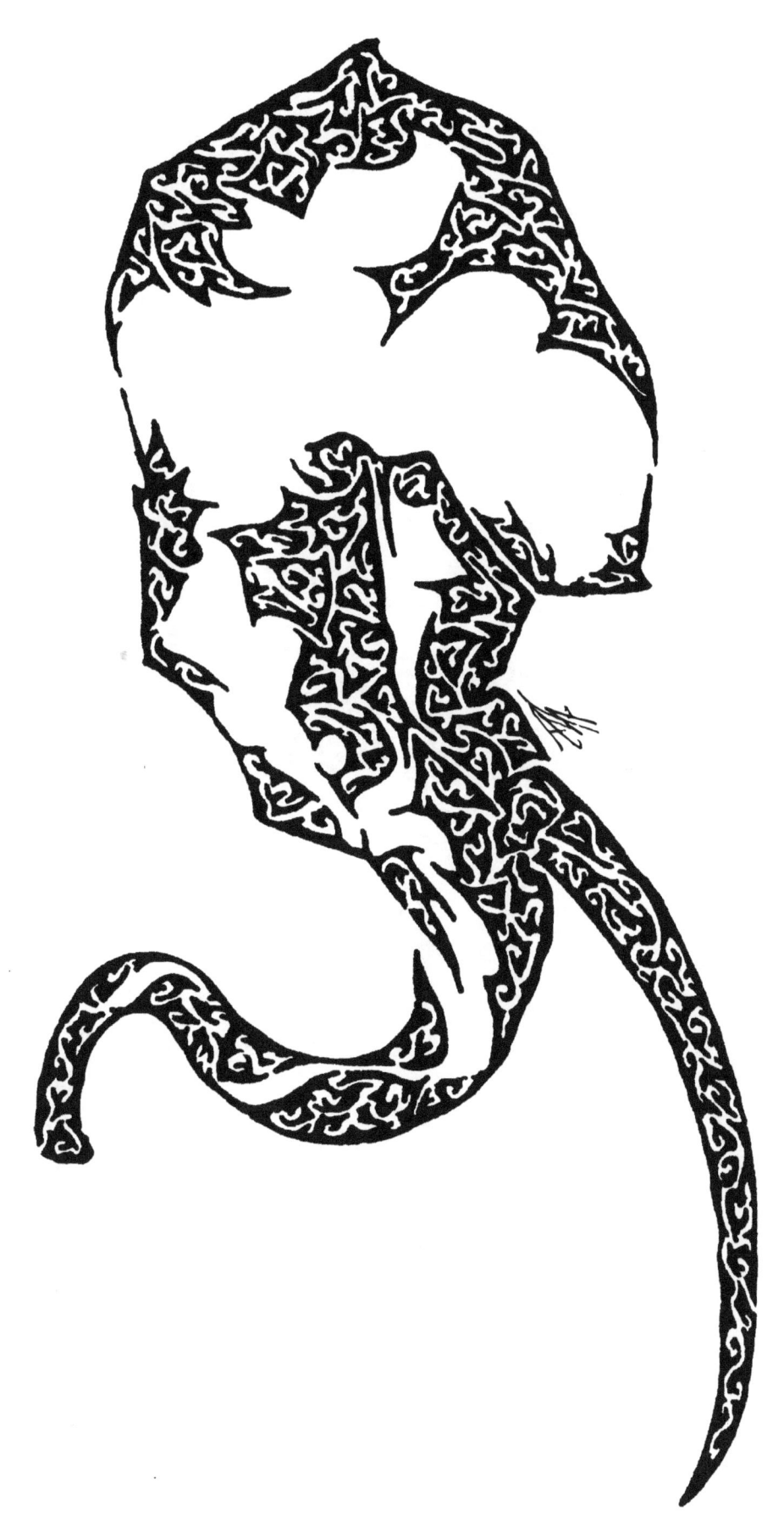

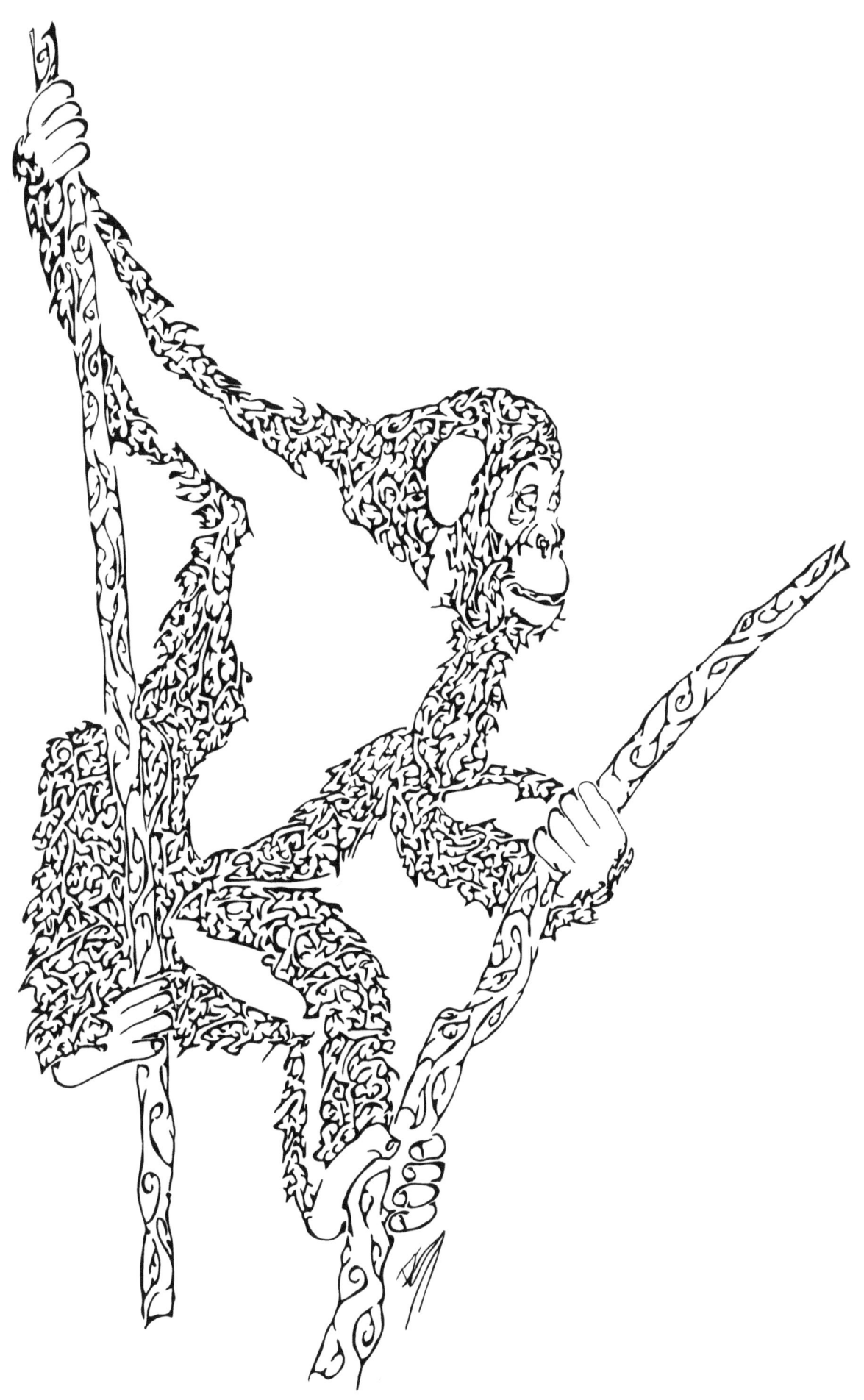

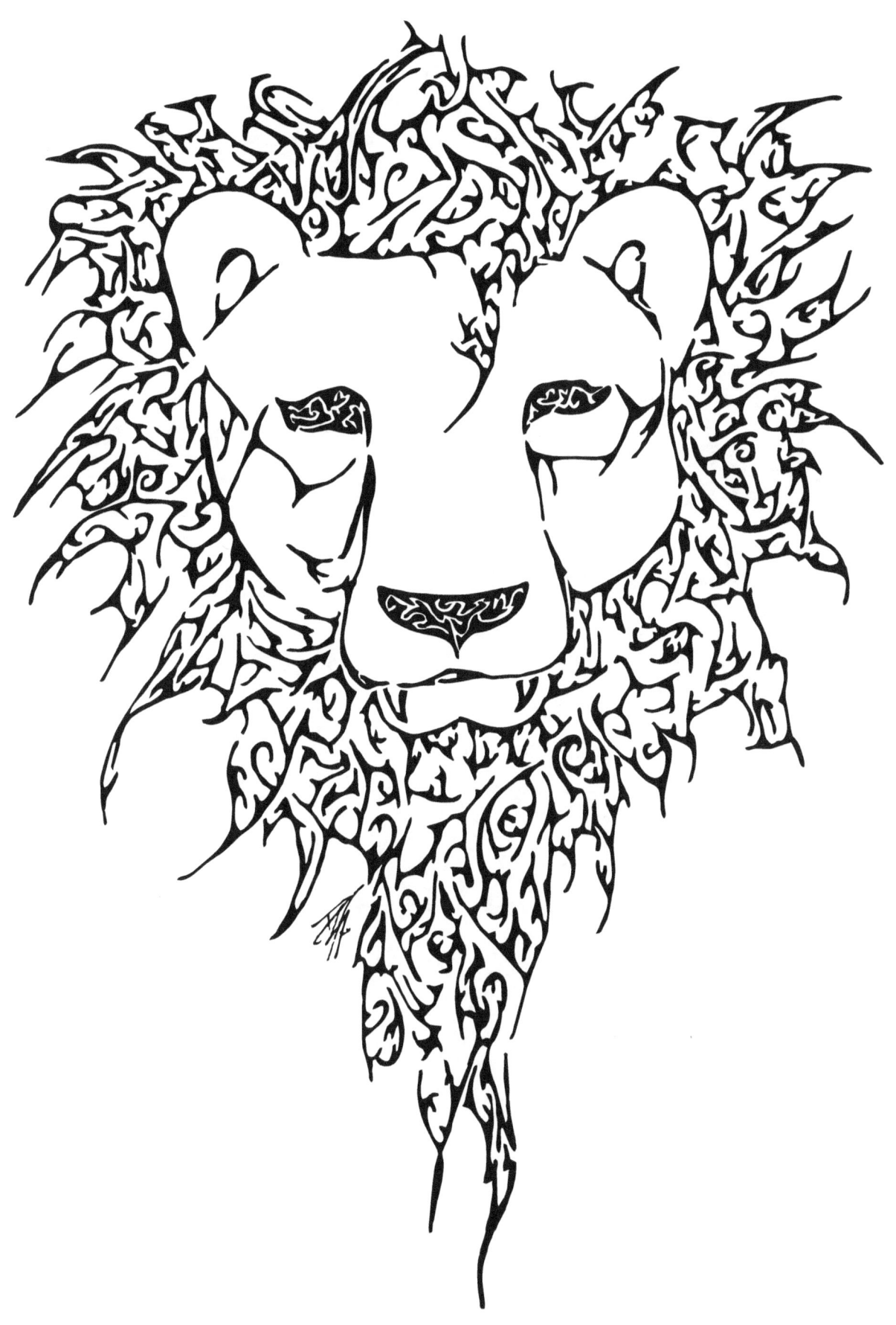

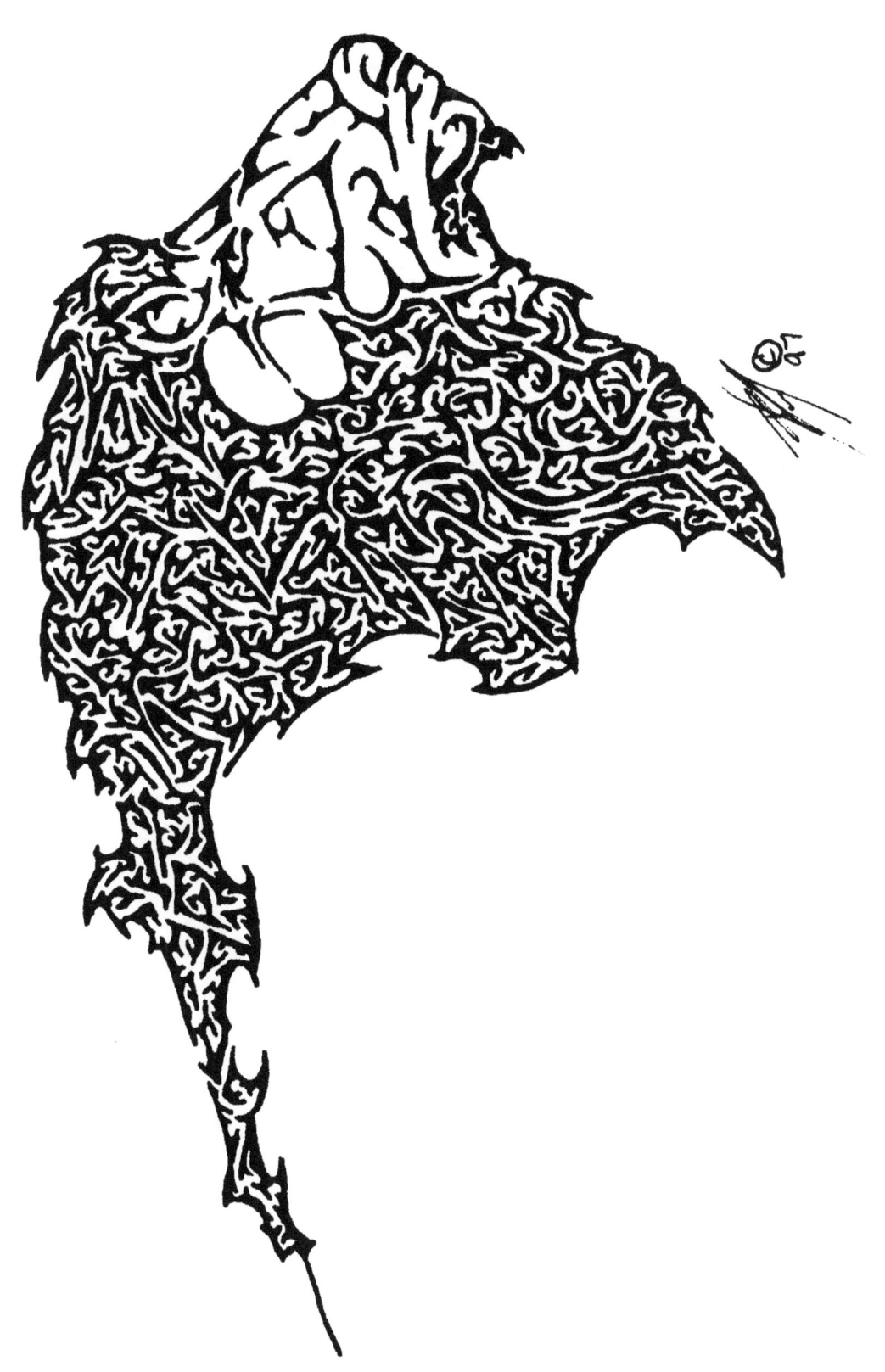

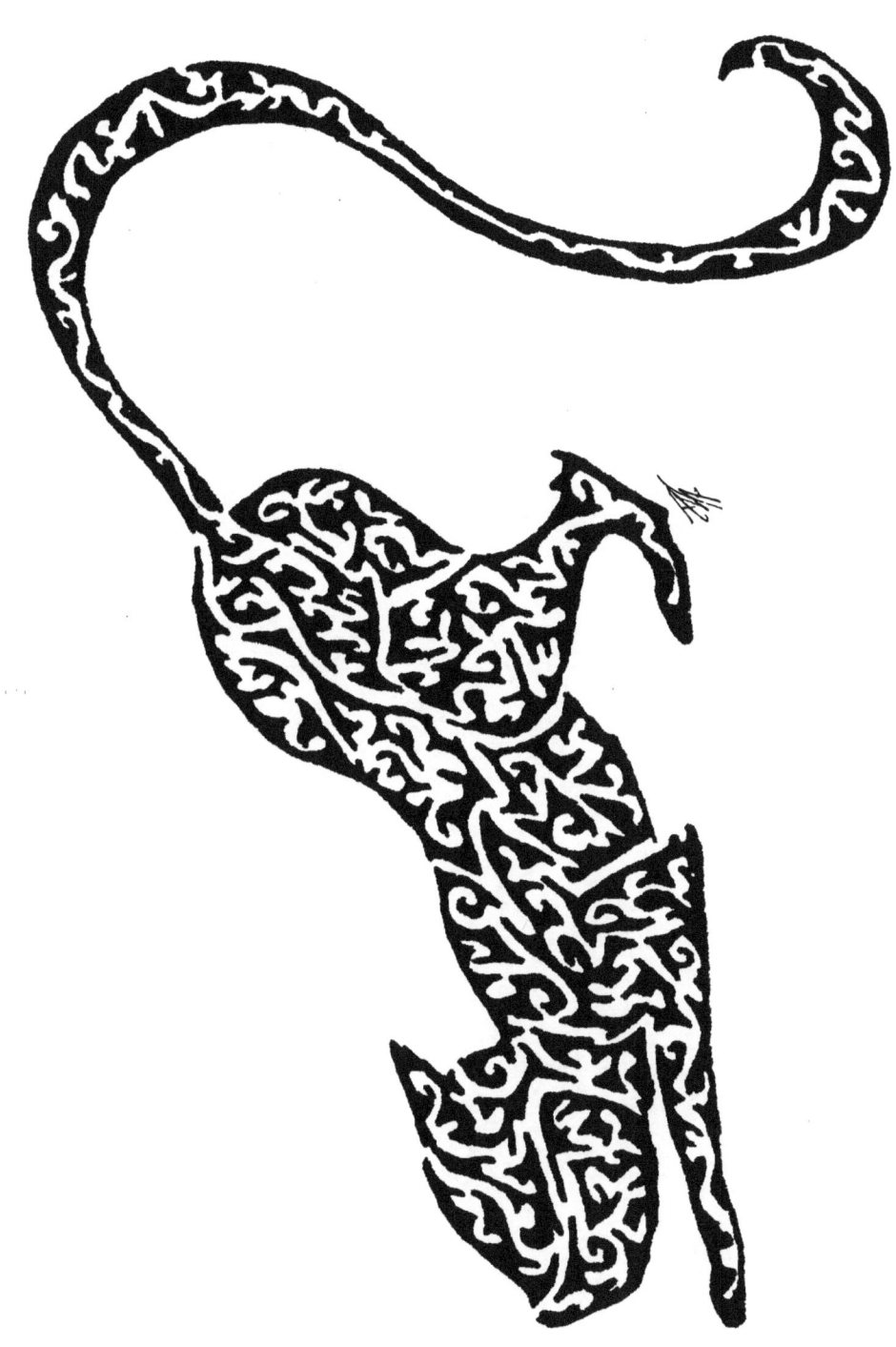

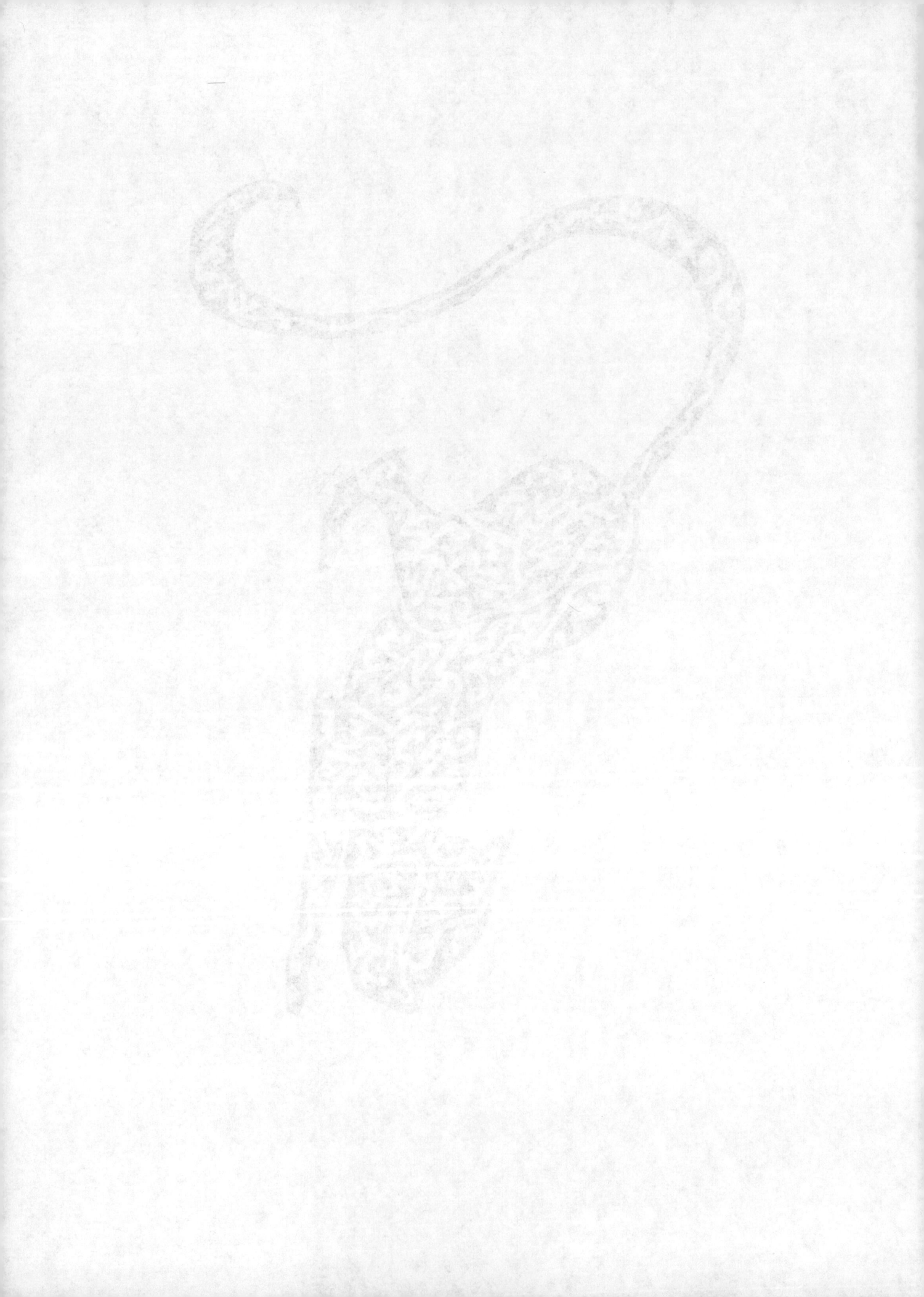

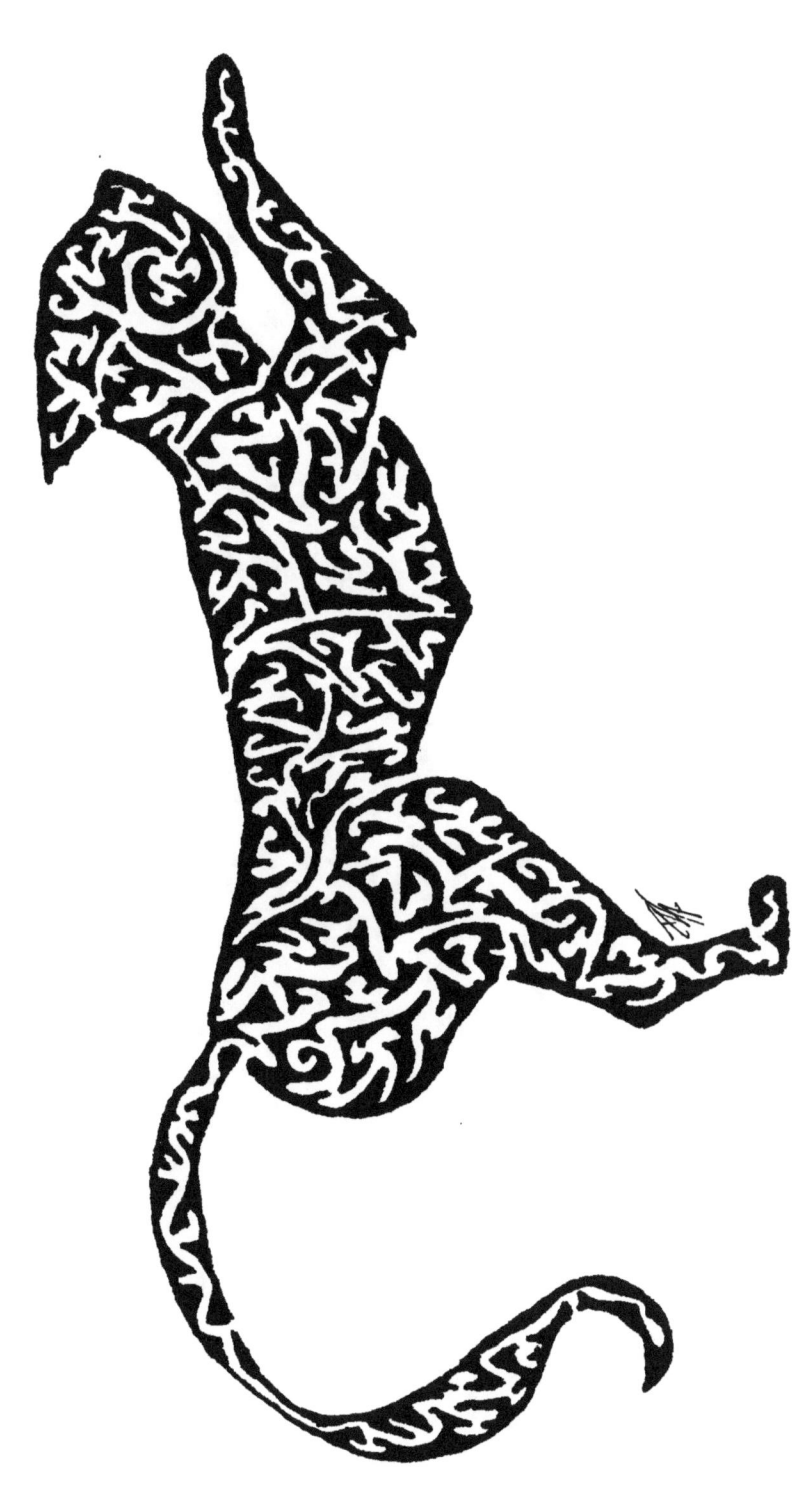

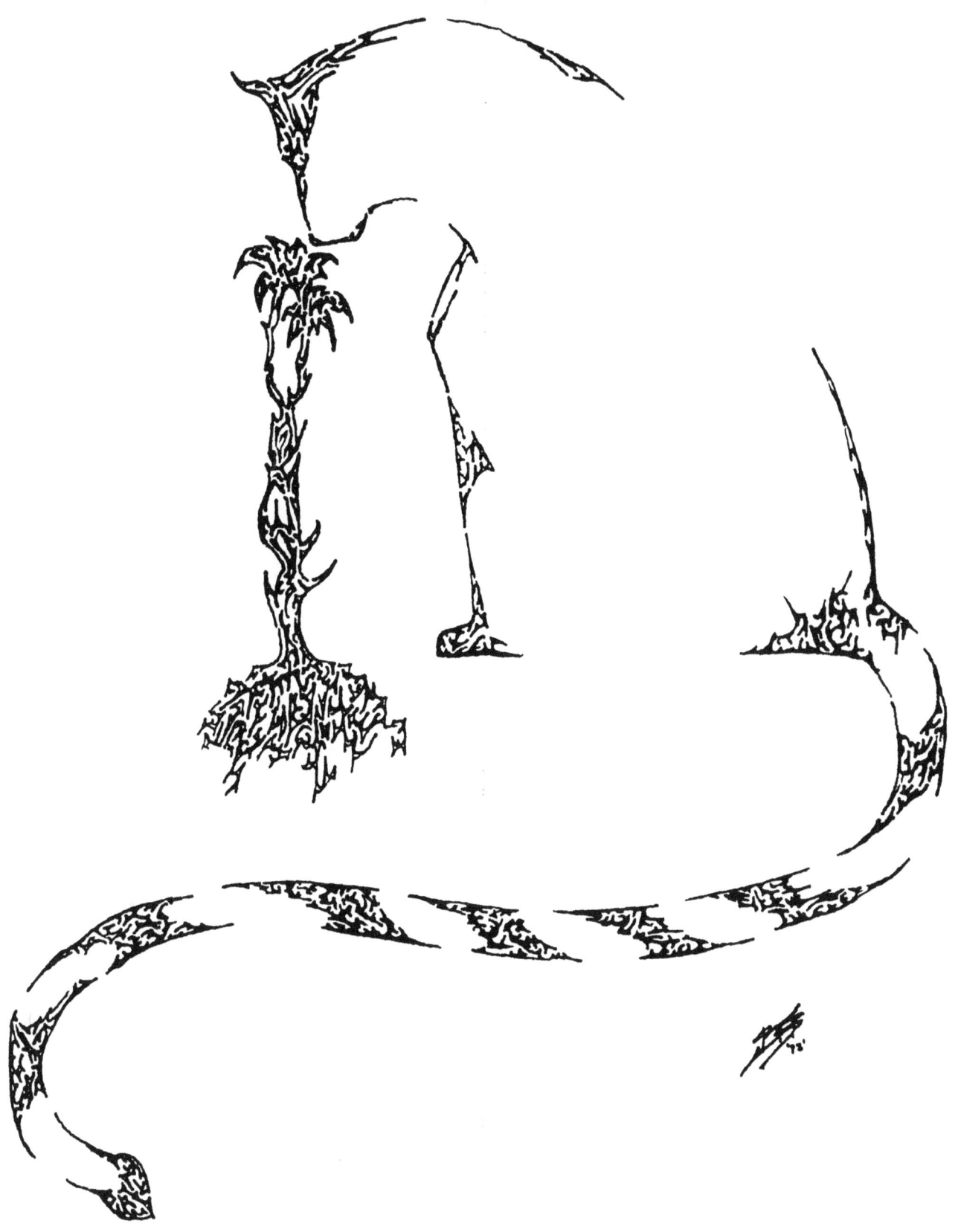

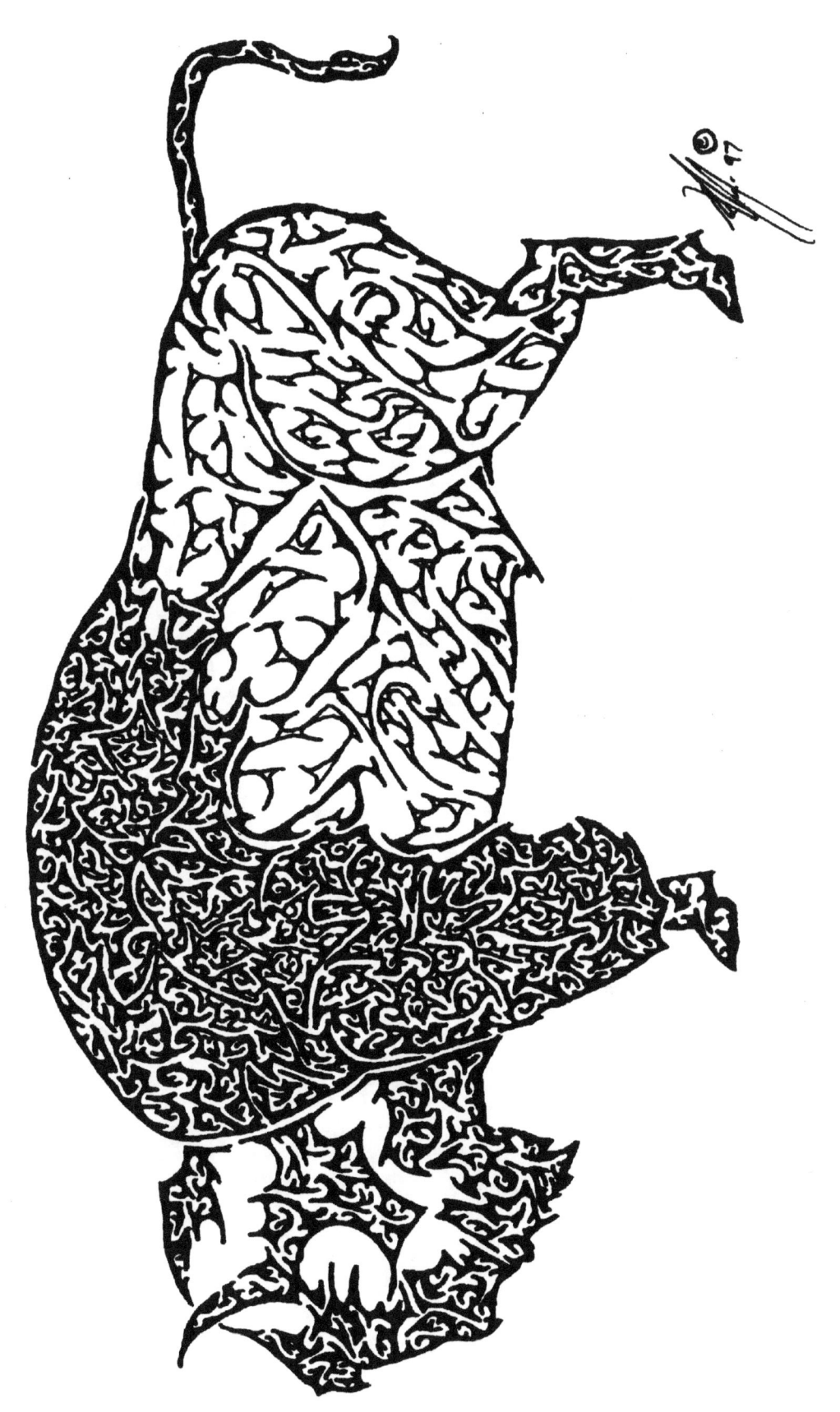

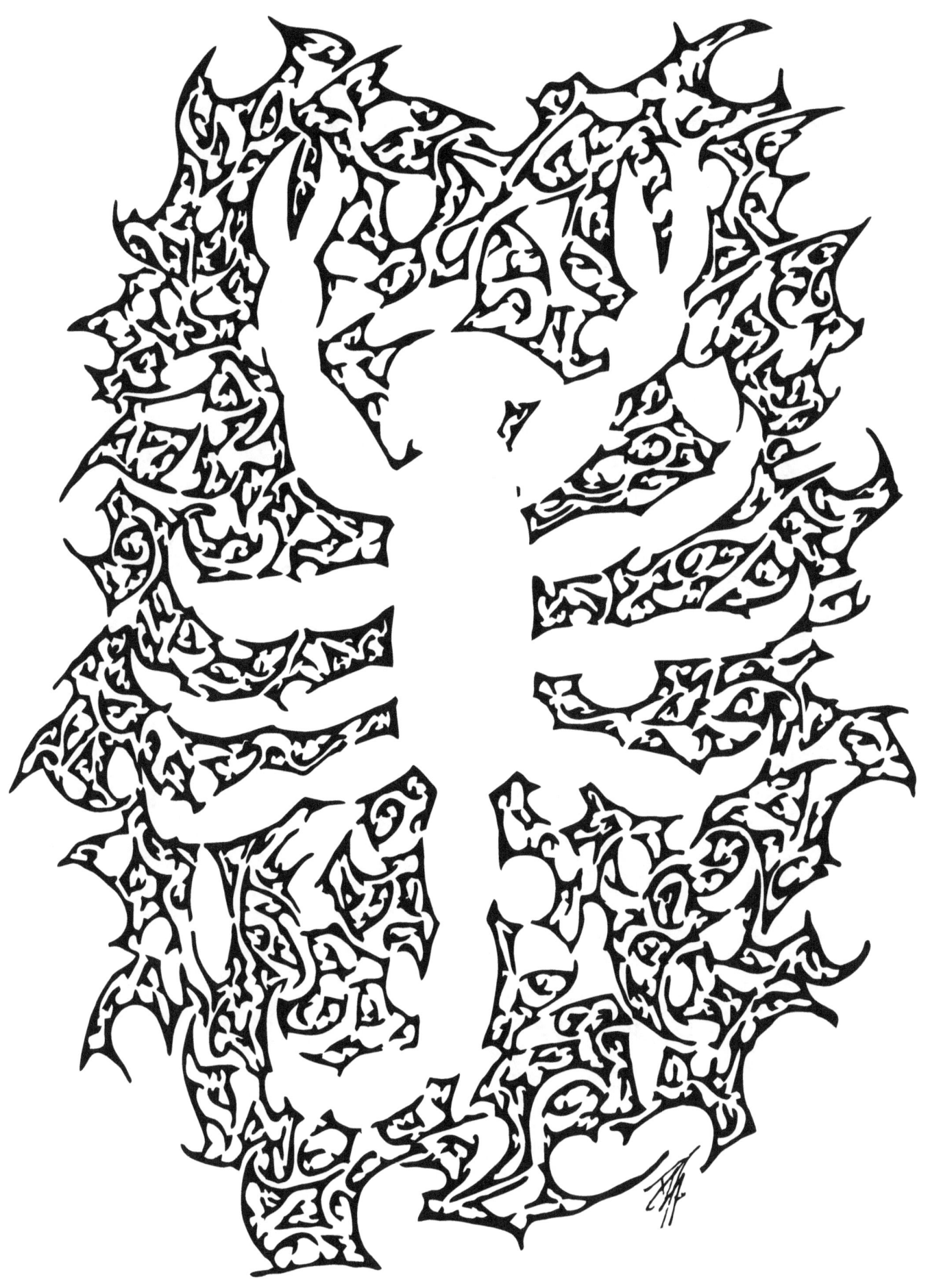

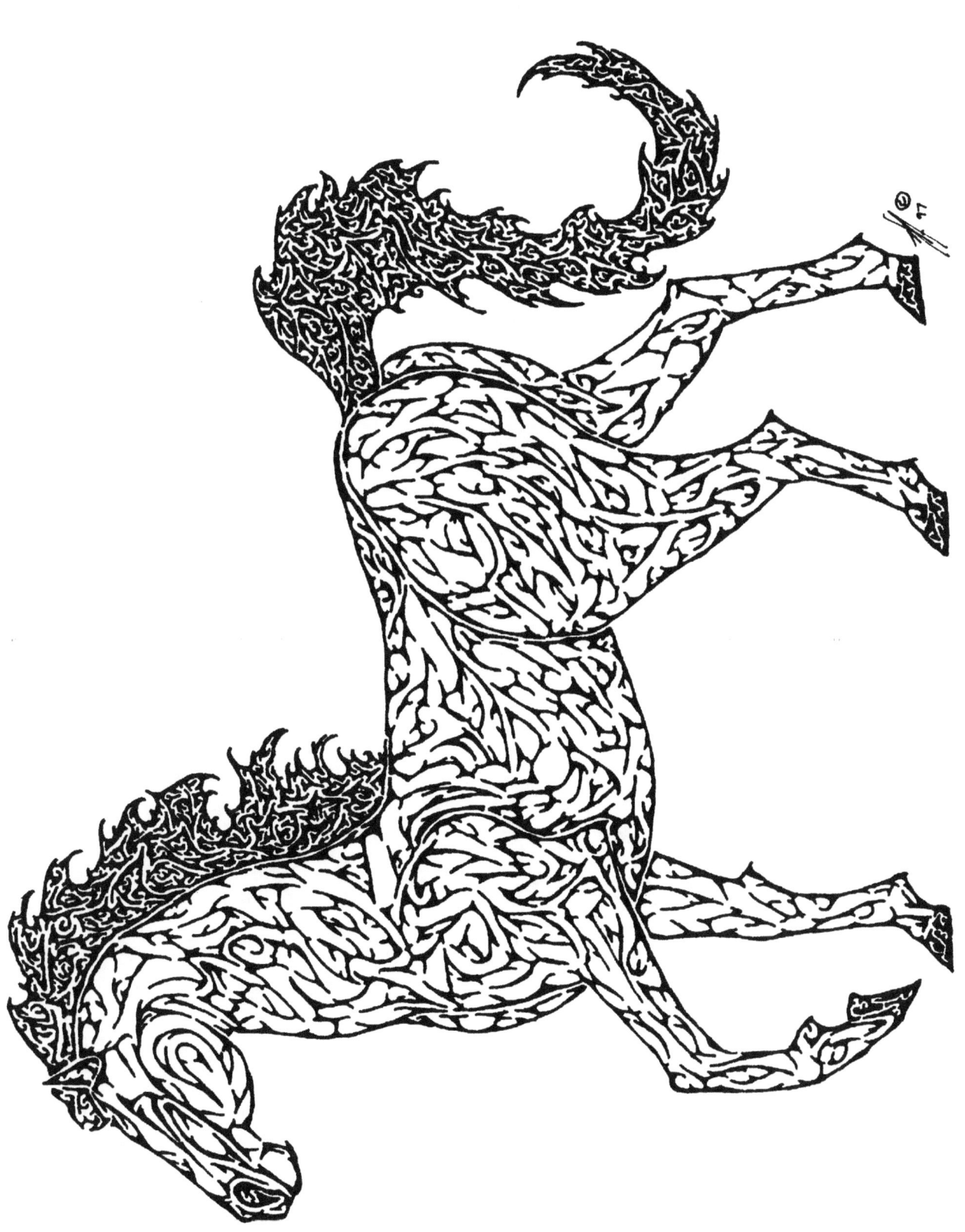

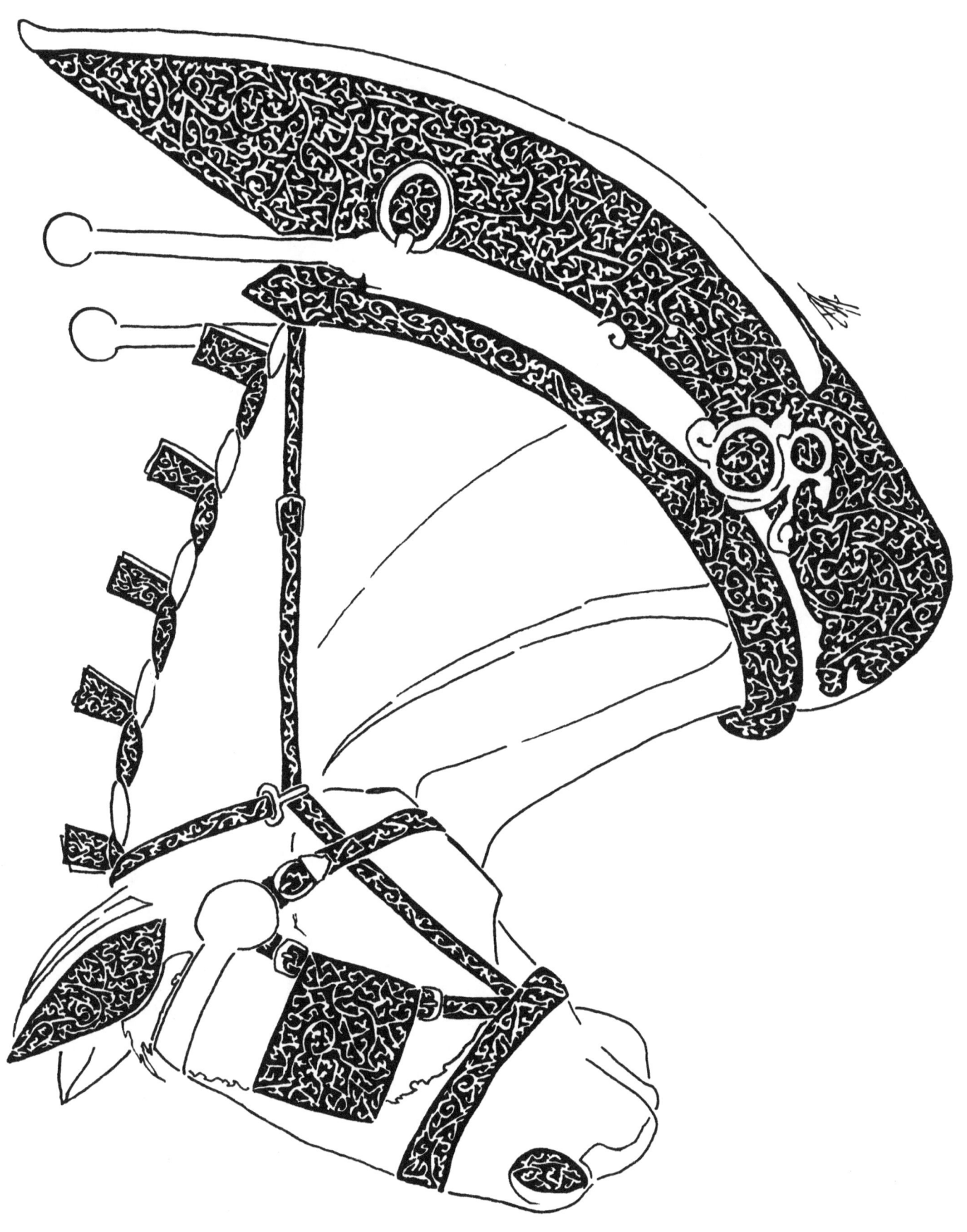

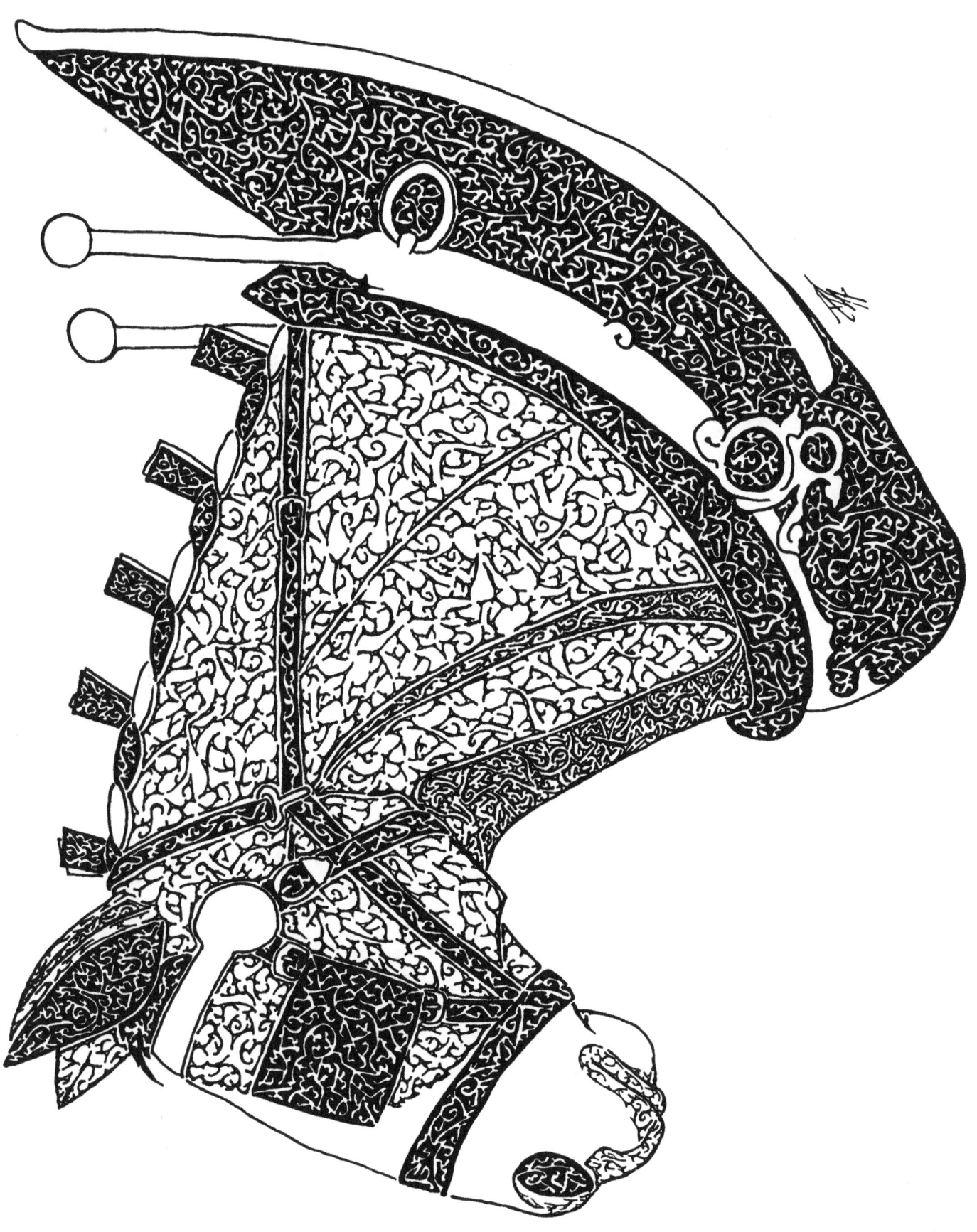

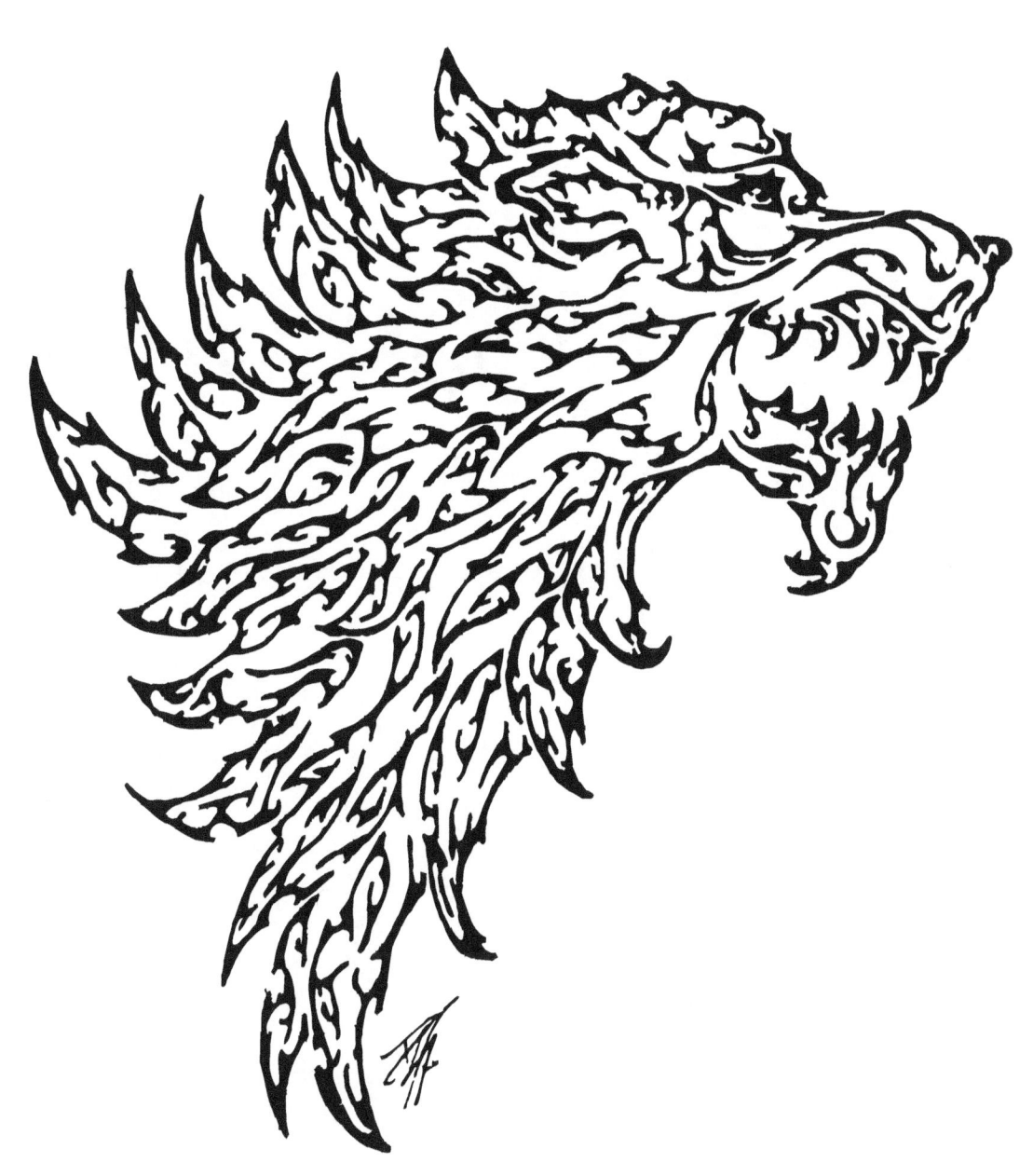

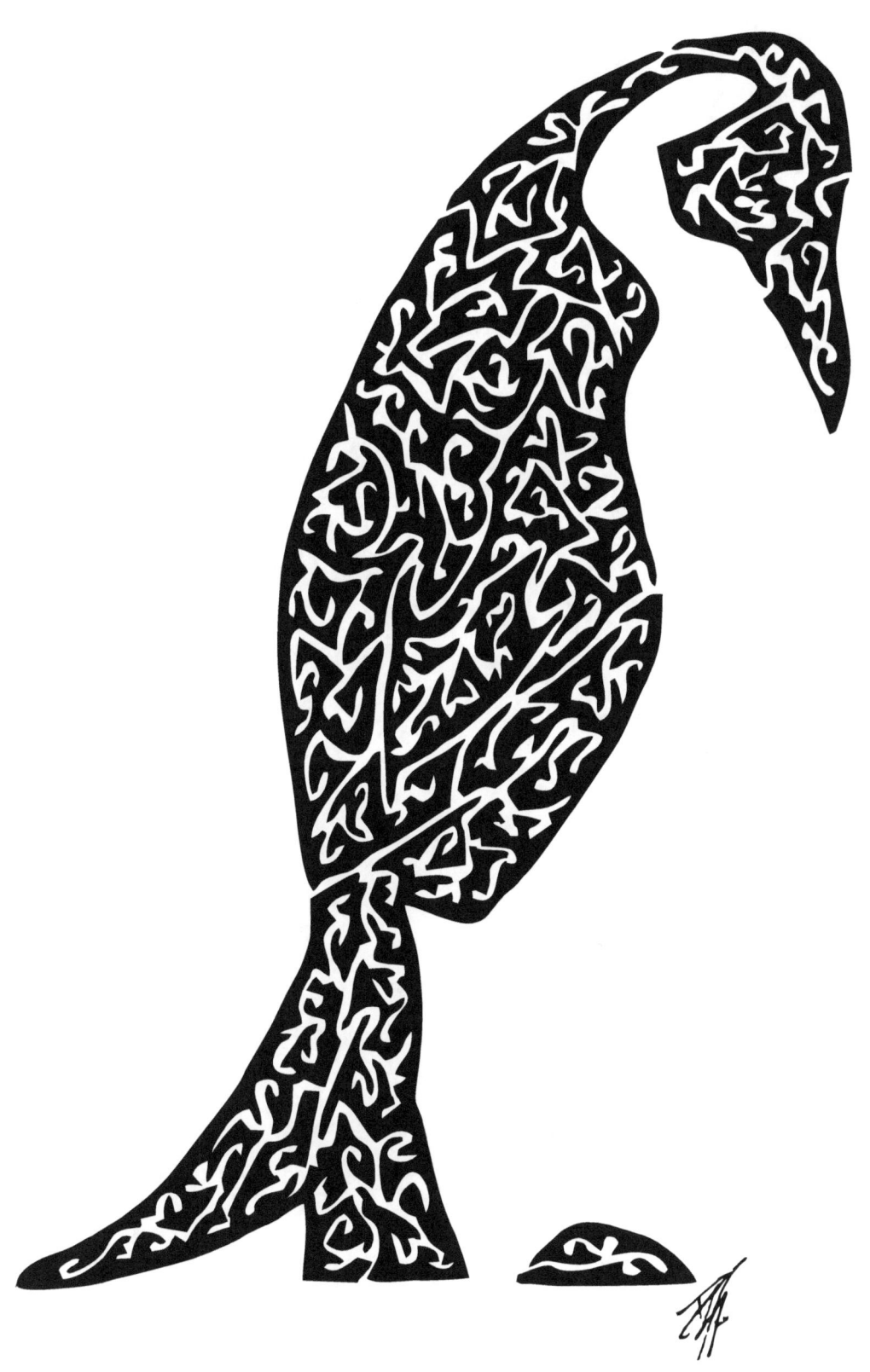

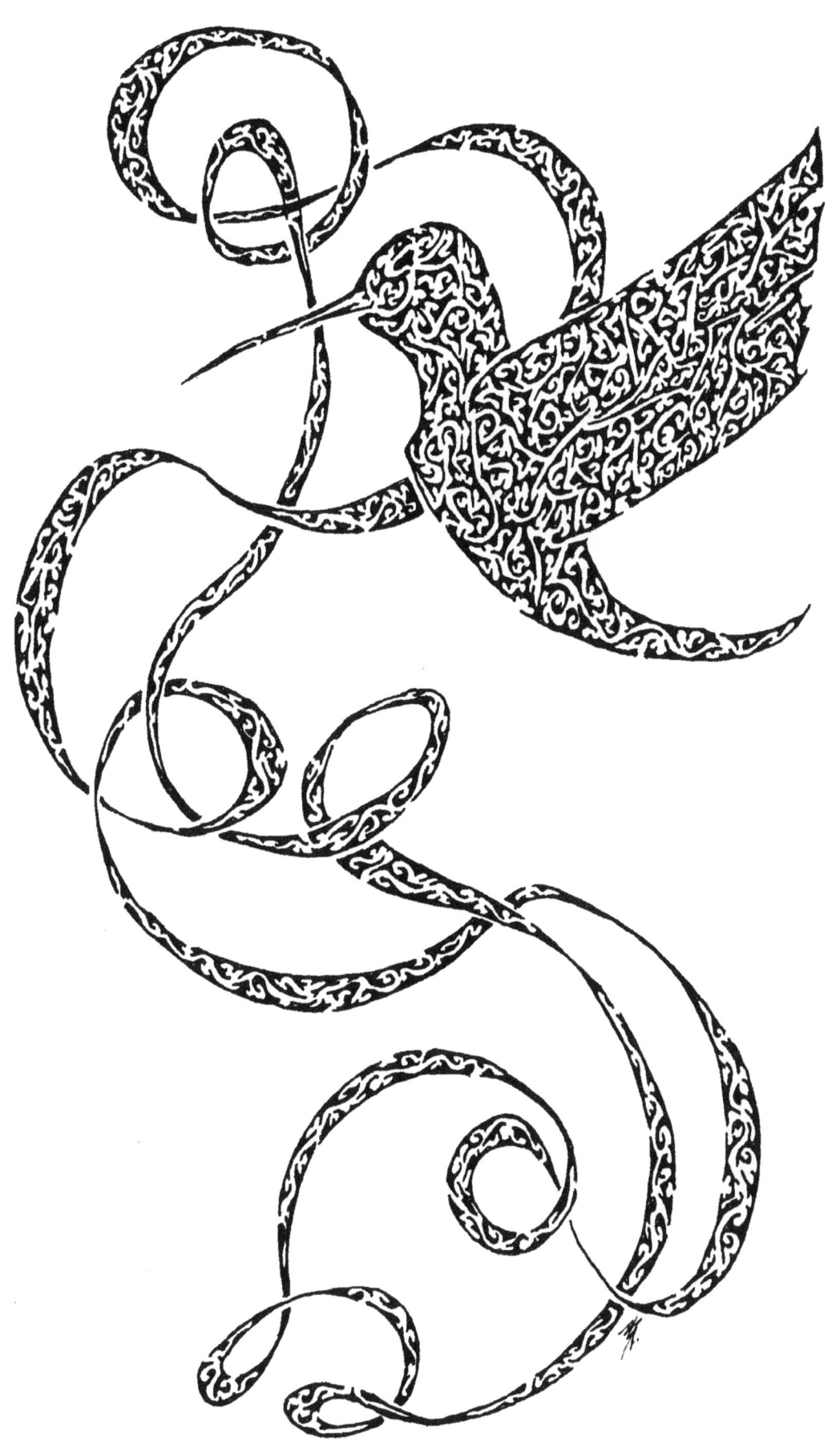

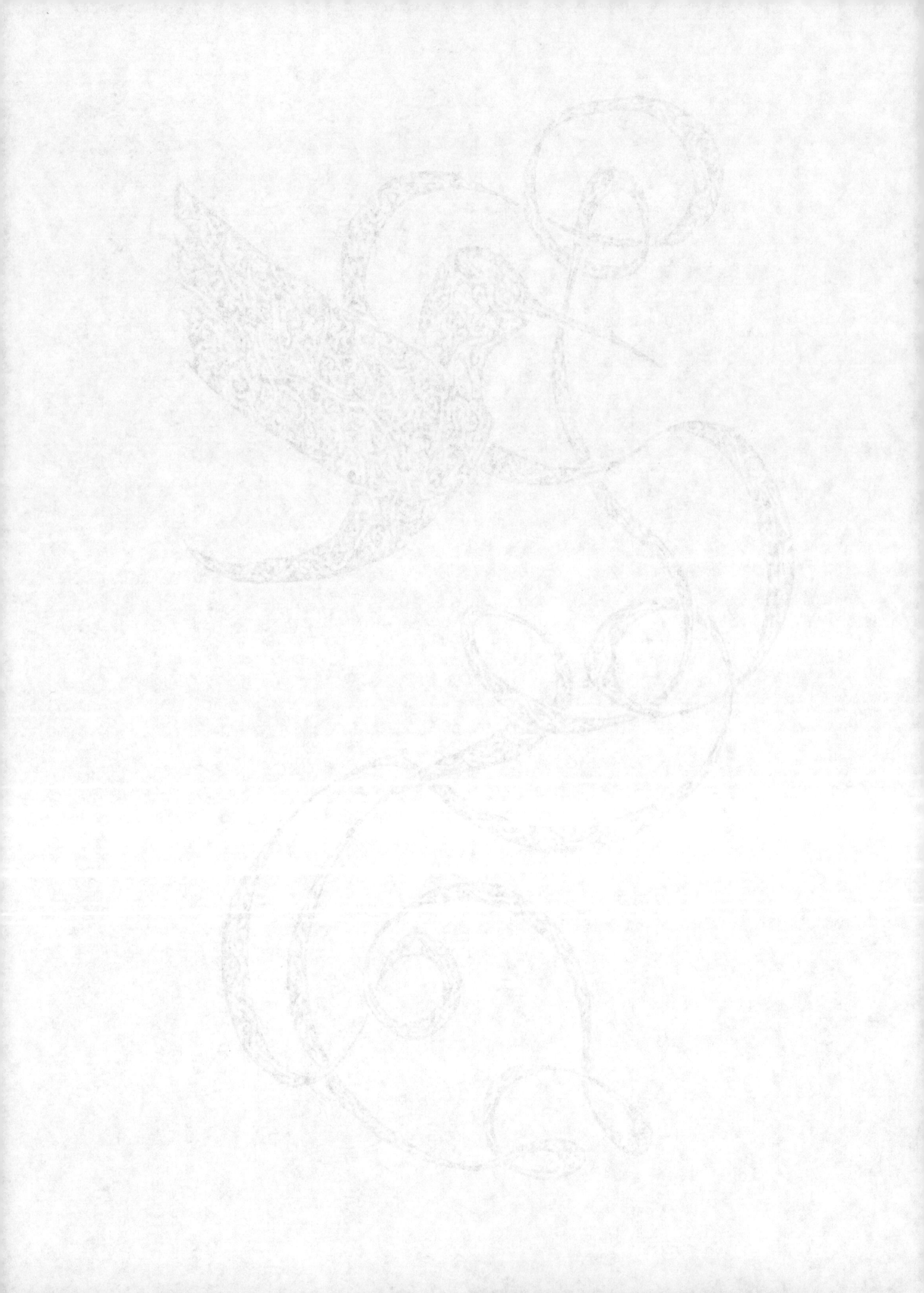

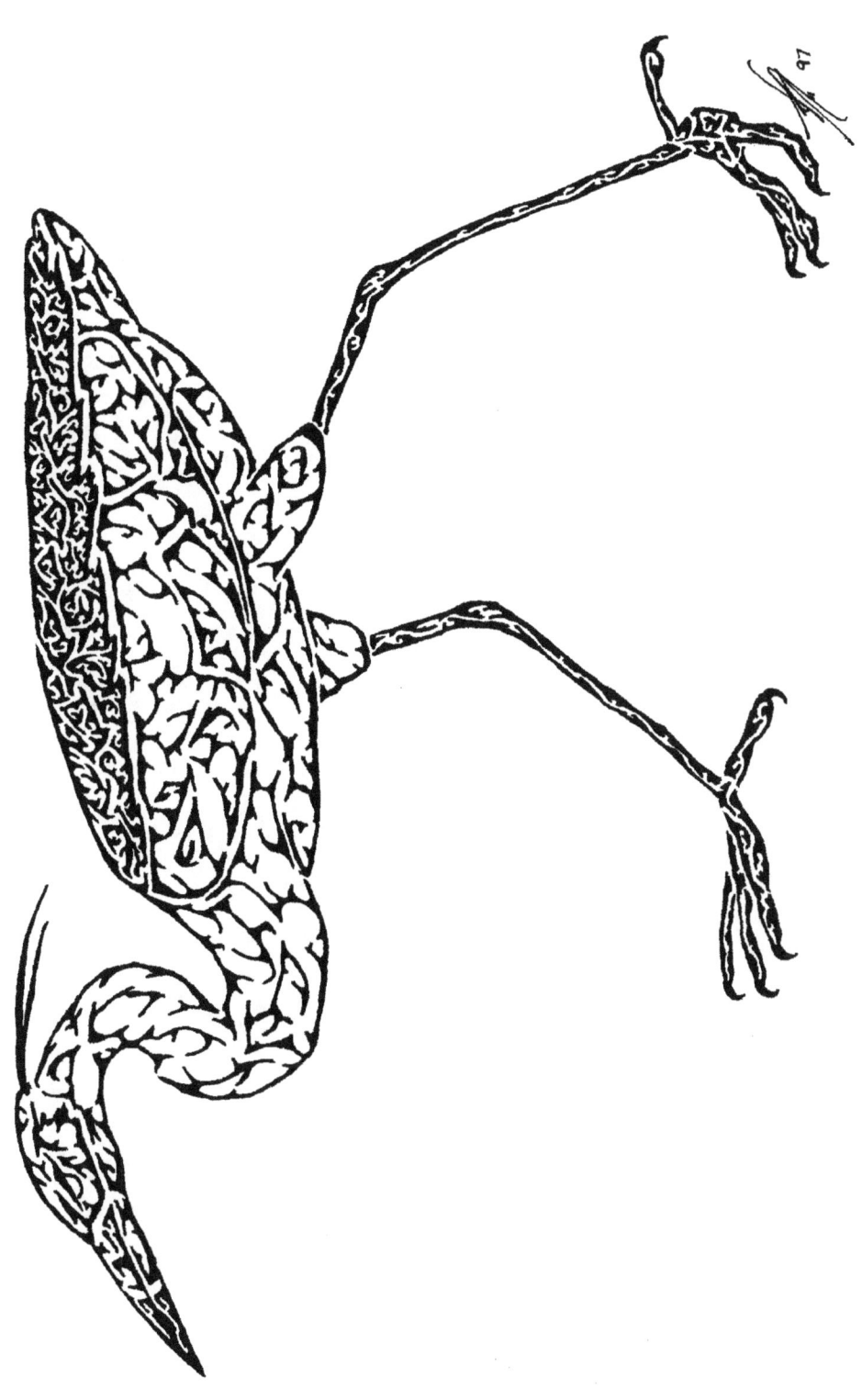

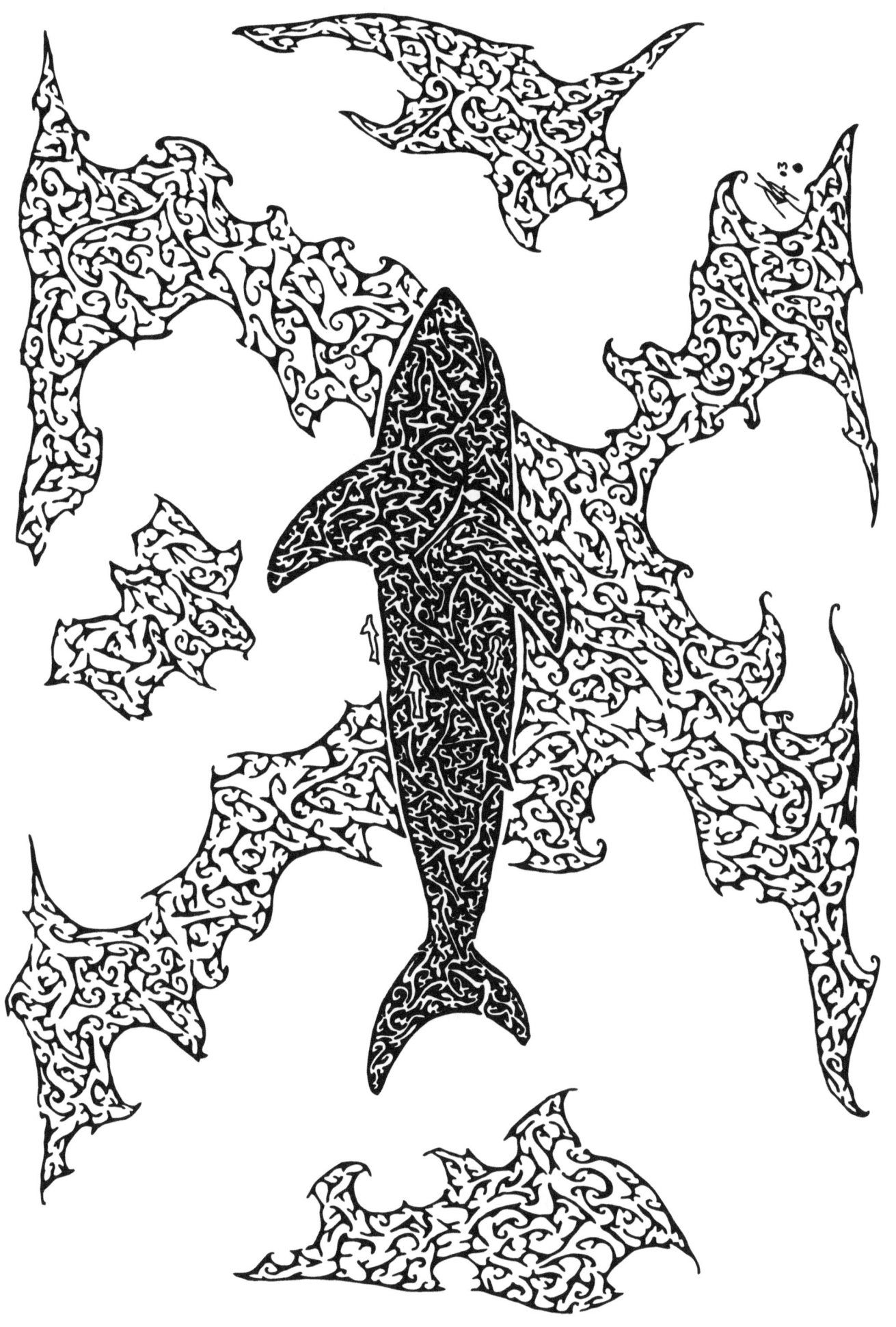

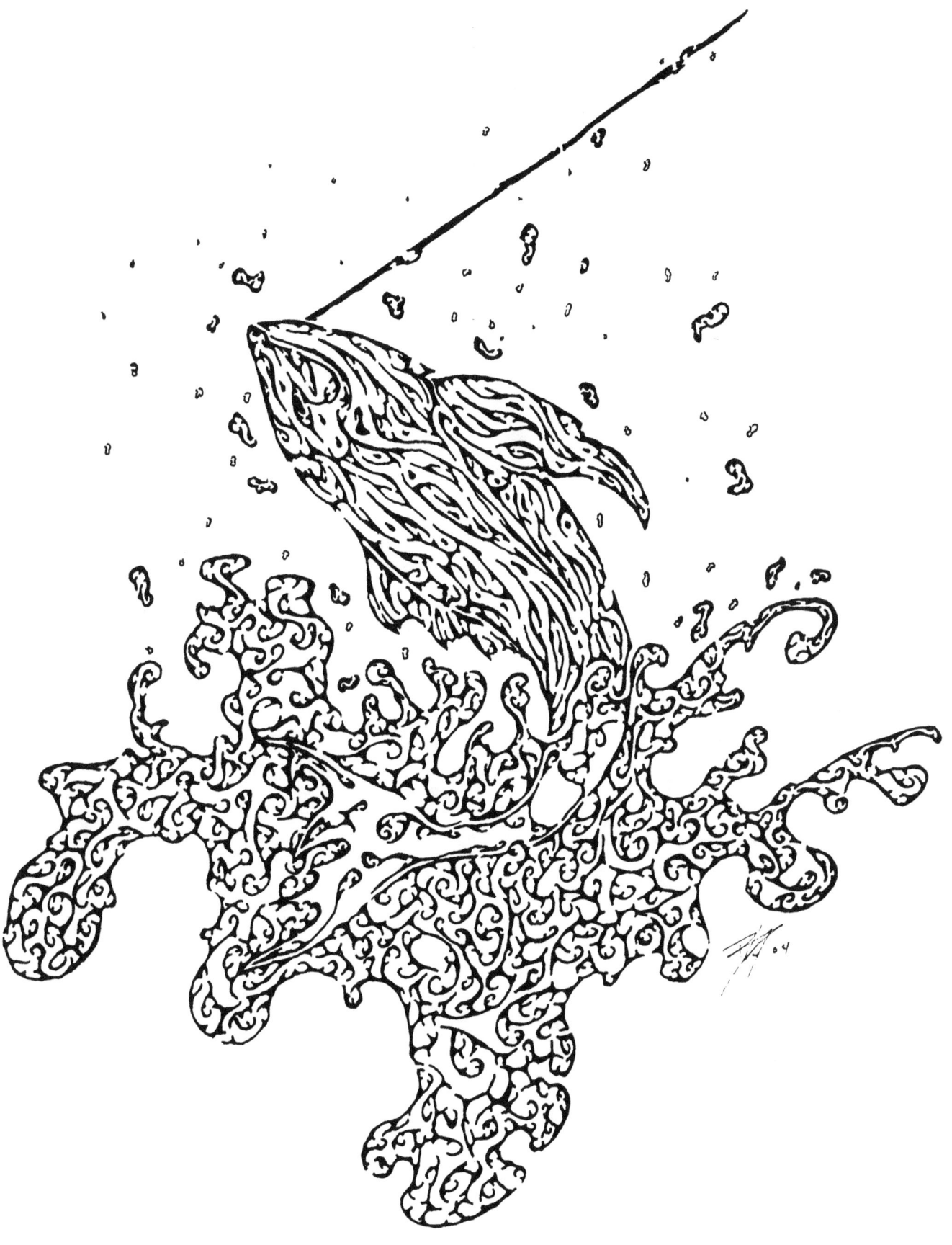

The testing page. The more watery the media
the more it will bleed thru the paper.

Coming Soon

FANTASY

Volume 4

INSPIRED ART

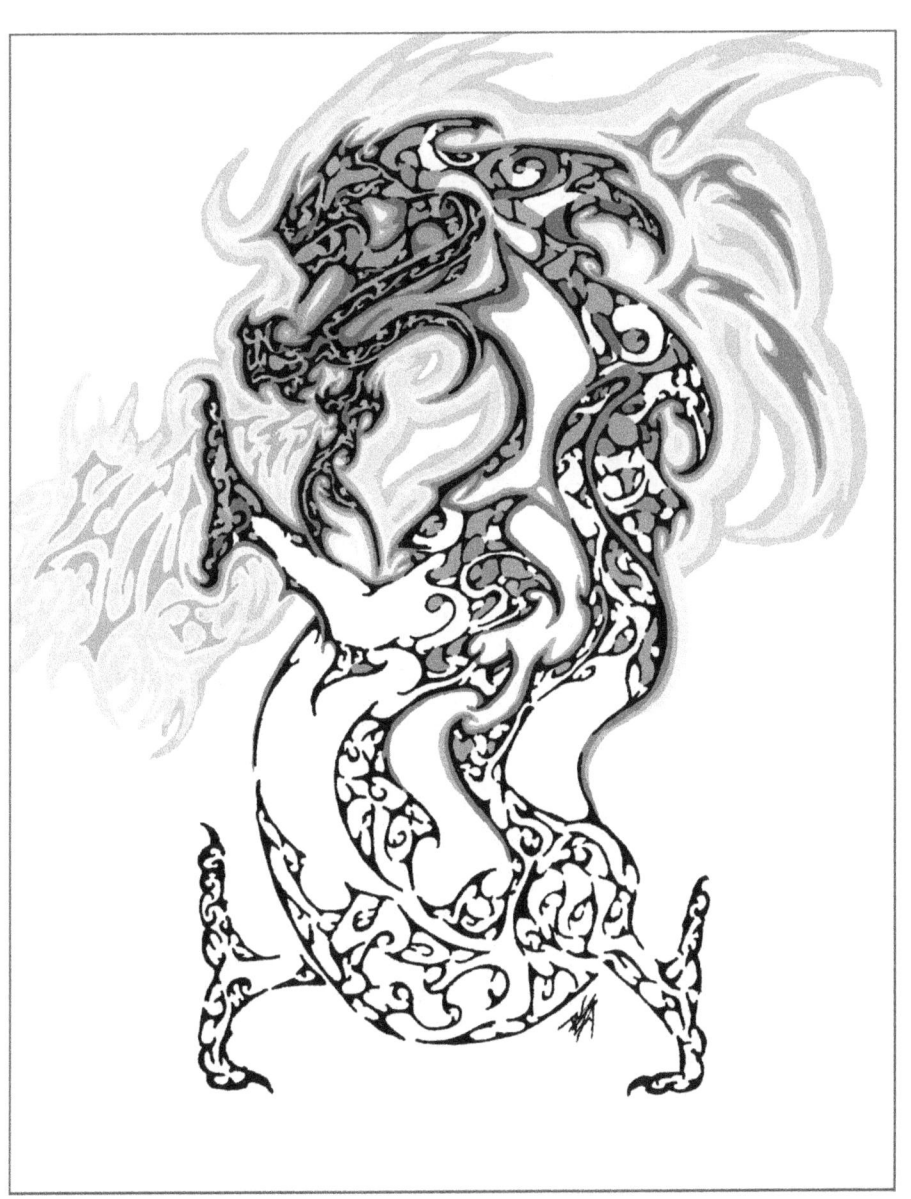

Adult Coloring book by Brian Scott

The testing page. The more watery the media the more it will bleed thru the paper.

Giraffe

Water Buffalo

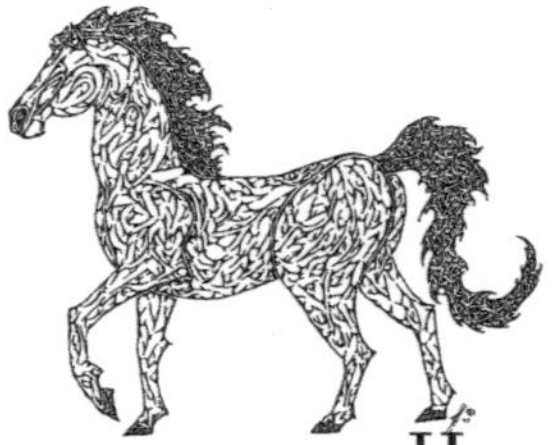

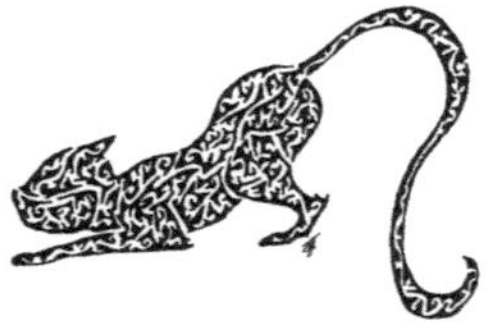

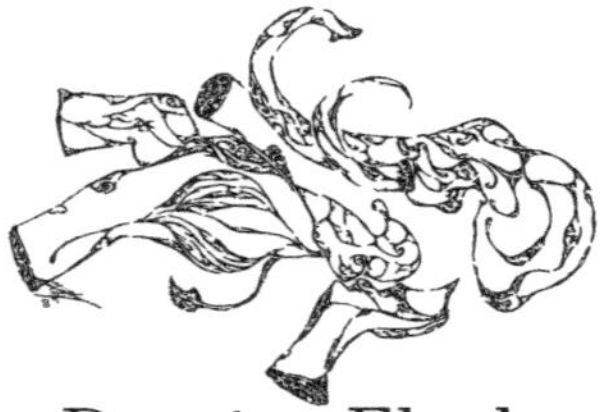

Rino

Rino

Rino

Dancing Elephant

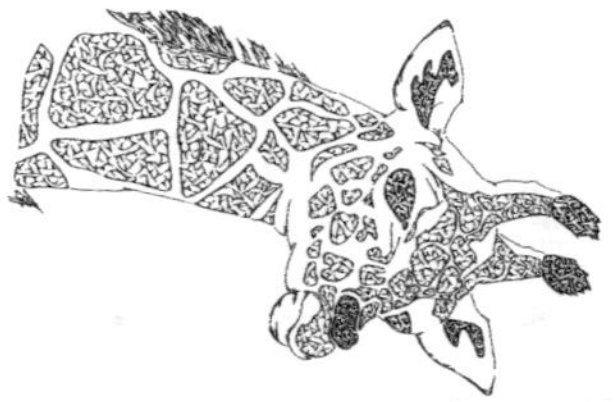

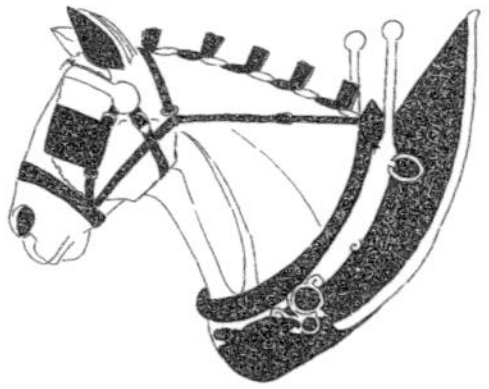

Elephant Head

Monkey

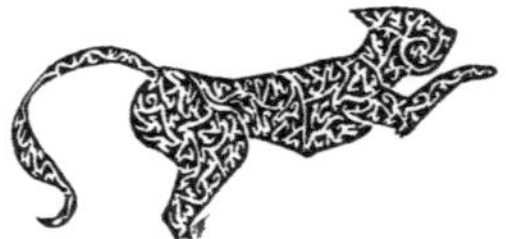

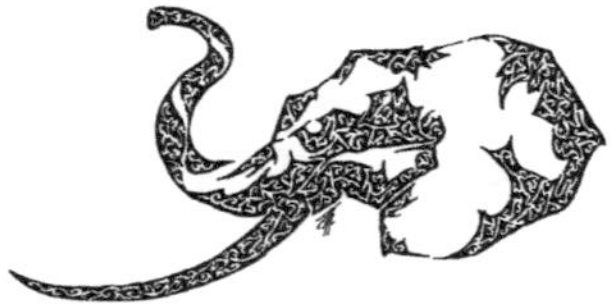

Lion

Lion

Cat

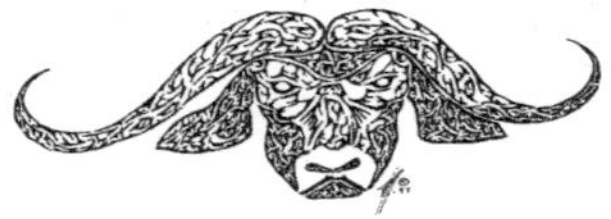

Cat

Cat & Flower

Buffalo

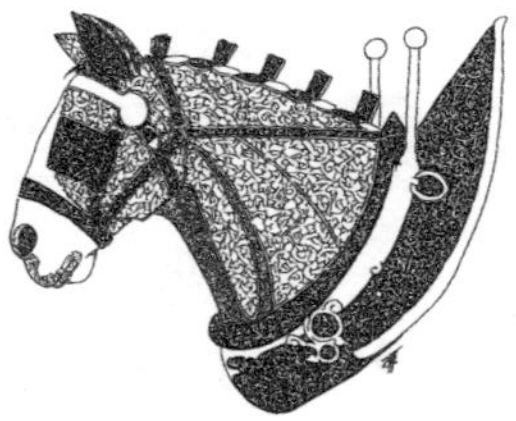

Scorpion

House

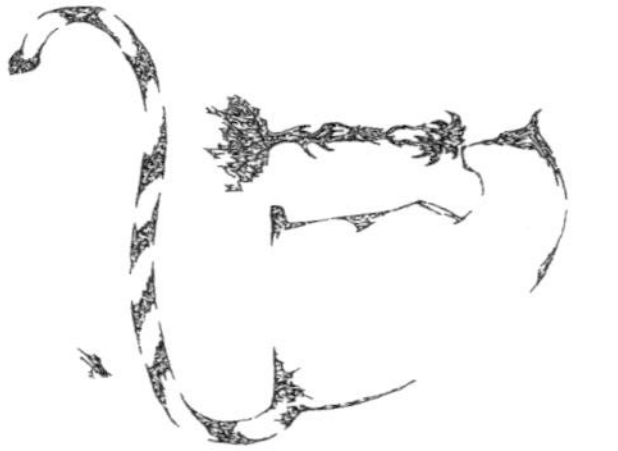

Clidsdale Horse

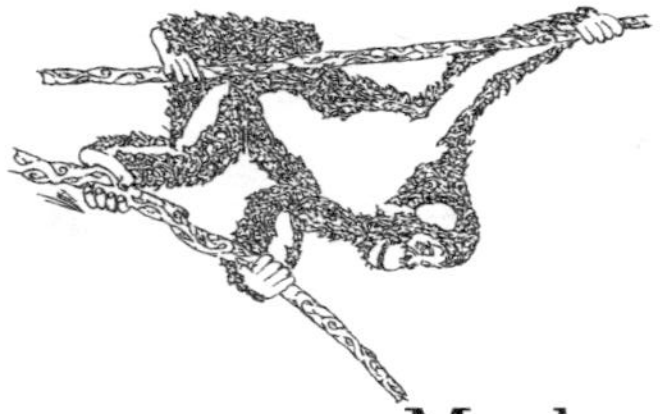

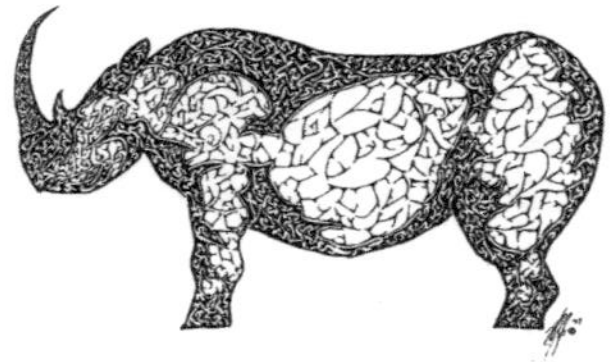

Clidsdale Horse

Wolf

Penguin

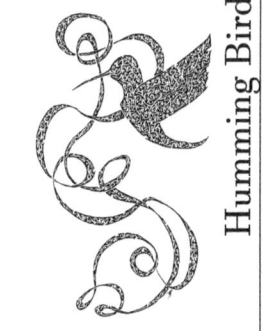

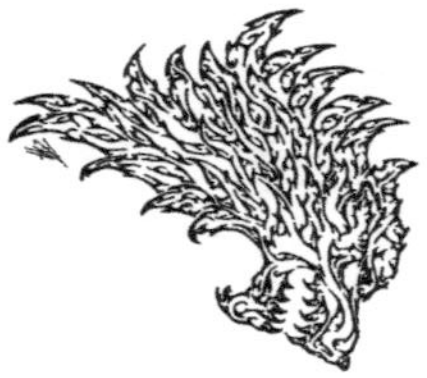

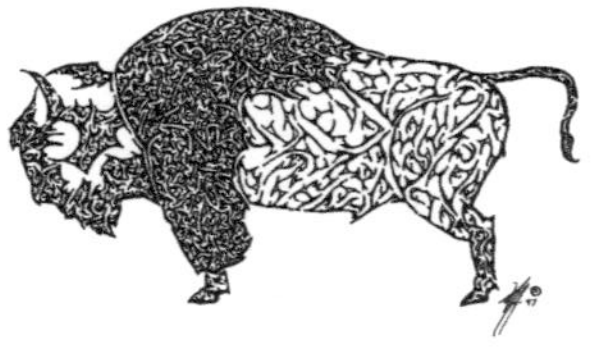

Humming Bird

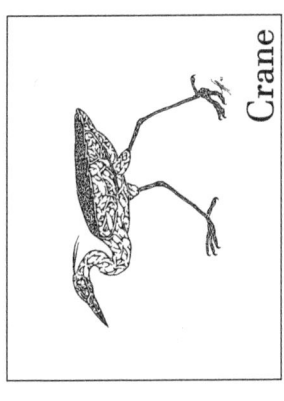

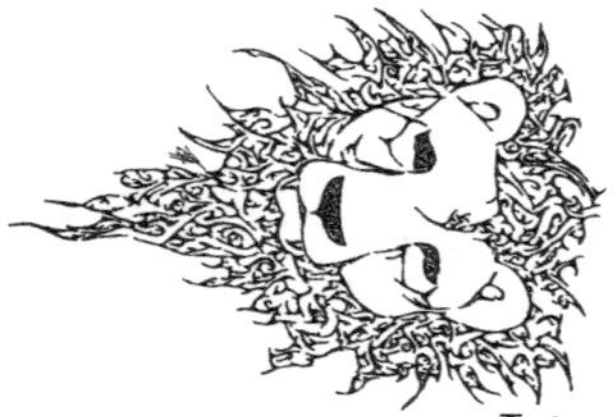

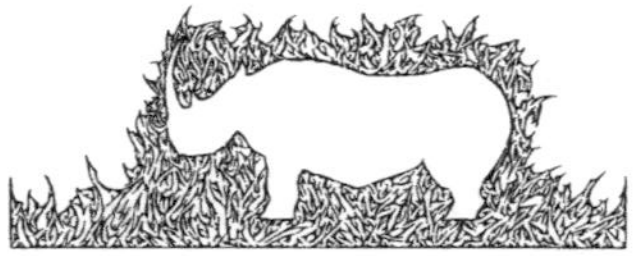

Crane

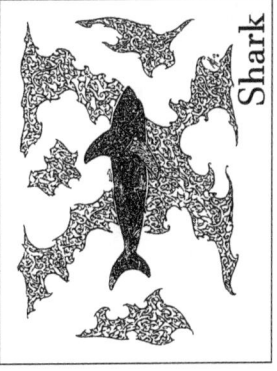

Shark

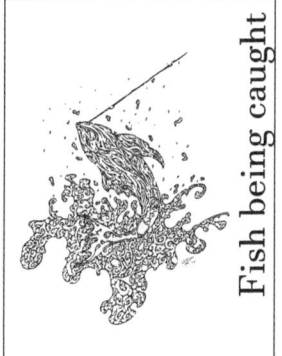

Fish being caught

Part of the:
Inspired Art
Coloring
Books
Series

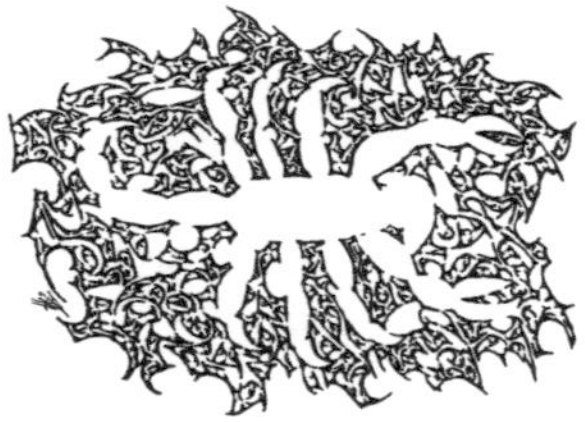

by Brian Scott

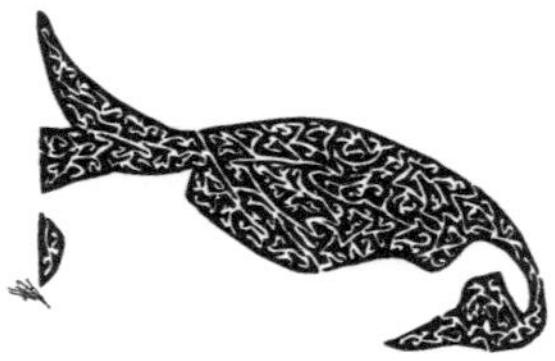

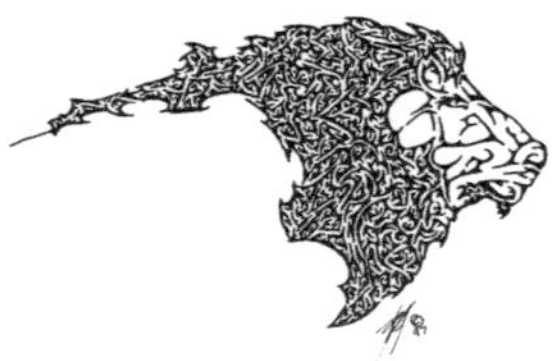

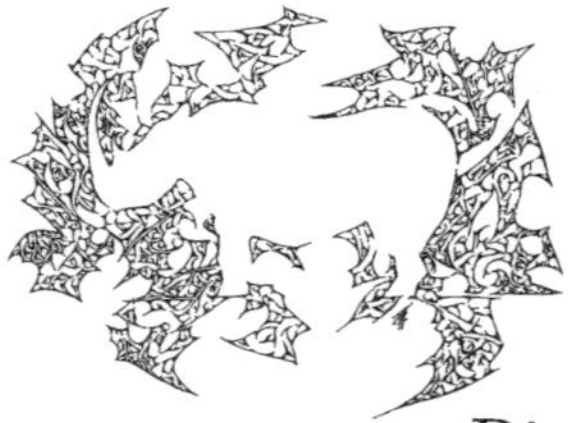

Enjoy more of my art in my other coloring books

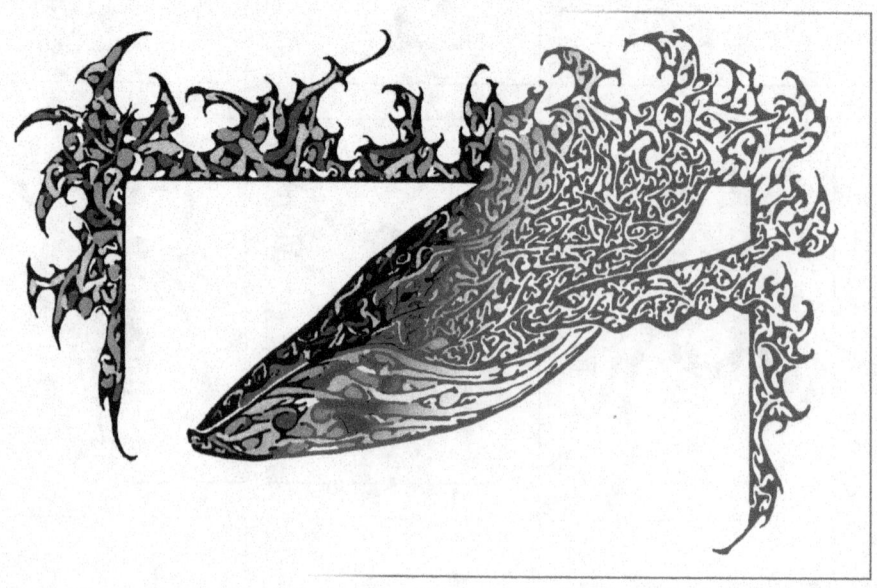

ALASKA INSPIRED ART

Adult Coloring book by Brian Scott

Volume 1

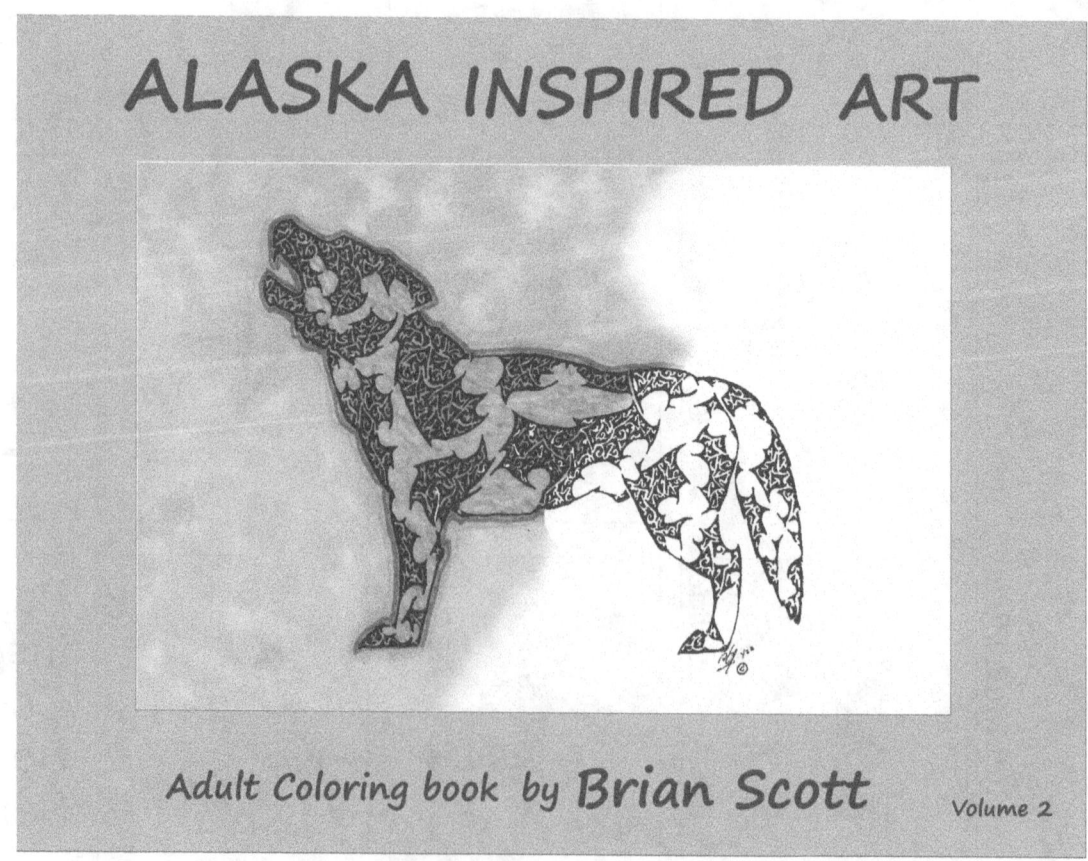

ALASKA INSPIRED ART

Adult Coloring book by Brian Scott

Volume 2

www.ingramcontent.com/pod-product-compliance
Lightning Source LLC
Chambersburg PA
CBHW080552190526

45169CB00007B/2745